THE OTHER SIDE
OF THE STORY

THE OTHER SIDE
OF THE STORY

Structures and Strategies
of Contemporary
Feminist Narrative

Molly Hite

Cornell University Press

ITHACA AND LONDON

First published 1989 by Cornell University Press.
First printing, Cornell Paperbacks, 1992.

International Standard Book Number 0-8014-2164-0 (cloth)
International Standard Book Number 0-8014-8017-5 (paper)
Library of Congress Catalog Card Number 89-776

Printed in the United States of America

Librarians: Library of Congress cataloging information appears on the last page of the book.

⊗ The paper in this book meets the minimum requirements of the American National Standard for Information Sciences—Permanence of Paper for Printed Library Materials, ANSI Z39.48-1984.

For Patricia G. Hite and F. Herbert Hite

Contents

Acknowledgments

Scholarship never takes place in a vacuum, and feminist criticism is a particularly populous enterprise, both because of the cooperation it encourages and because of the generosity of spirit distinguishing its individual practitioners. I am especially grateful to Mary Jacobus, Sydney Janet Kaplan, and Ann Snitow for reading and commenting on this manuscript in several versions. Thanks also to Miriam Amihai, Rachel Blau DuPlessis, Henry Louis Gates, Jr., Gayle Greene, Alison Lurie, and Scott McMillin, who read and commented on one or more individual chapters. Temma Berg, Tucker Farley, Philip Brian Harper, Tamar Katz, Diane McPherson, Deborah Rosenfelt, Claire Sprague, and Barbara Szmyd offered ideas that I happily incorporated. Gwen Bird was an able research assistant on the Margaret Atwood chapter, and Frederick Muratori was unfailingly patient in helping me negotiate the labyrinth of the Cornell University Library system. The American Council of Learned Societies and the College of Arts and Sciences at Cornell University provided leave and travel support. Bernhard Kendler of Cornell University Press proved predictably talented in finding exactly the readers this manuscript needed, among them Brenda Silver and Patricia Yaeger. Gerard Cox proved once again my most assiduous reader and critic. Finally, I am indebted to the various organizations where I have found feminist criticism to be most successfully institutionalized: the National Women's Studies Association, the Modern Language Association, the Northeast Modern Language Association (with special thanks to its Women's Caucus), the Doris Lessing Society, and most of all the Cornell University English Department, whose members encouraged and supported this work from its beginnings.

Passages from *Lady Oracle* by Margaret Atwood, copyright © 1976 by O. W. Toad, Ltd, are used by permission of Simon & Schuster, Inc.; the Canadian Publishers, McClelland and Stewart, Toronto; and Andre Deutsch Ltd. Quotations from *The Golden Notebook* by Doris Lessing, copyright © 1962, 1990 by Doris Lessing, appear by permission of Simon & Schuster, Inc., and Michael Joseph Ltd. Passages from *After Leaving Mr. Mackenzie* by Jean Rhys, copyright 1931 by Jean Rhys, are reprinted by permission of HarperCollins Publishers, Inc., and Anthony Sheil Associates Ltd.

MOLLY HITE

Ithaca, New York

THE OTHER SIDE
OF THE STORY

Introduction

This book began with a question I first formulated some years ago in all innocence: Why don't women writers produce postmodernist fiction?

Like so many questions of the "Why don't women . . . ?" variety, this one initially seemed both straightforward and plausible, which is to say, neither particularly ambiguous nor particularly implicated in a network of masculinist assumptions. As far as ambiguity went, the possibility had not occurred to me. I meant by the question something fairly simple: it appeared evident to the point of being a truism that the important male fiction writers of the period after 1960 were characteristically engaged in certain kinds of stylistic and structural innovation and that the important female fiction writers of the period were engaged in no sort of innovation at all. If this assessment of the situation of contemporary writing now strikes me as so naïve that it amounts to purblind complicity, I will add that whenever I brought up my "Why don't women writers . . . ?" question—most often in feminist critical circles—people not only took my meaning in exactly the way that I had intended it, but responded with great interest, "Yes, why don't they?" and immediately began to propose possible answers. I suspect that I would get the same kinds of response today from many people, including many feminists.

Of course, addressing the question forced me to move rapidly from "Why don't they . . . ?" to "What *do* they do?" at which point a whole other world opened up, the other side of this particular metanarrative about how men and women write. This book contends that a number of the most eminent and influential women writing in the contemporary period are attempting innovations in narrative form that are *more* radical in their implications than the dominant modes of fictional experiment, and more radical precisely inasmuch as the context for innovation is a critique of a culture and a literary tradition apprehended as profoundly masculinist. But I did not end up trying to admit a select group of female—and feminist—writers to the emergent canon of postmodernism. I now believe that one reason Jean Rhys, Doris Lessing, Alice Walker (whom I consider in relation to her literary progenitor Zora Neale Hurston), and Margaret Atwood have not been more widely regarded as innovative narrative strategists is that they seem, as a group, recognizably distinct from the postmodernists: equally concerned with the languages of high and low culture, for instance, but differently implicated in these languages, similarly aware of the material and cultural conditions of their own writing but calling attention to this status in more complicated and more ideologically charged ways.[1] In particular, experimental fictions by women seem to share the decentering and disseminating strategies of postmodernist narratives, but they also seem to arrive at these strategies by an entirely different route, which involves emphasizing conventionally marginal characters and themes, in this way *re*-centering the value structure of the narrative.[2]

This claim for the highly experimental nature of recent women's

[1]Brian McHale, *Postmodernist Fiction* (New York: Methuen, 1987), offers an intelligent and accessible overview of the conditions and defining features of the postmodernist narrative—and establishes in addition the masculine and maculinist characteristics of this category of writing. My *Ideas of Order in the Novels of Thomas Pynchon* (Columbus: Ohio State University Press, 1983) aims to situate Pynchon as an exemplary postmodernist and, to this end, discusses implications for narrative of specifically modernist and postmodernist ontological premises. See especially pp. 3–10 and 13–45. Although I am explicitly concerned here with four widely read and widely accepted female writers, my list is in no way intended to be exhaustive. A few of the writers (in English) whose fictions also belong under the rubric of contemporary feminist narrative are Kathy Acker, Christine Brooke-Rose, Angela Carter, Michelle Cliff, Elizabeth Jolley, Toni Morrison, Grace Paley, Joanna Russ, and Fay Weldon.

[2]I deal more explicitly with one instance of an "entirely different route" in "(En)Gendering Metafiction: Doris Lessing's Rehearsals for *The Golden Notebook*," *Modern Fiction Studies* 34, no. 3 (1988), 481–500.

writing may strike many readers as unusual—perhaps even outra-
geous—given the various institutional contexts within which we
read, describe, debate, evaluate, categorize and analyze contemporary fiction. But these contexts are no more innocent of masculinist
presuppositions than my original question, and they condition critical practices that lead us to read innovative fiction by women back
into a tradition that presumes women's writing is inherently conservative or flawed or both. Such contexts serve to mute female
difference, effectively intervening in women writers' attempts to
articulate what I call here the other side of the story.

I take it as a premise that it is possible to read other-wise, in ways
that acknowledge female-created violations of convention or tradition as deliberate experiments rather than inadvertent shortcom-
ings.[3] The silencing of female attempts to articulate an "other side"
to the dominant stories of a given culture is never complete, in that
this "side" is not in any absolute sense unimaginable or inconceiv-
able (or outside the Symbolic order, in Lacanian terms).[4] My readings
imply a somewhat different account—at once less drastic and more
political—not only of the relation of women to language but also of
the relation of the feminist writer to a narrative tradition that works
to inscribe her within its own ideological codes. I return briefly to
this issue at the conclusion of the book, at a point where I hope it
will be more evident that the key question for feminist narrative is
not "*Can* there be discursive practices that to some extent evade or
undermine masculinist presuppositions?" but "Given such discursive practices, under what conditions and using what strategies are
we most likely to *discern* them?"

Quite early in my reading, I found that I was appropriating the

---

[3]Important precedents for this contention and for my own methodology are Rachel
Blau DuPlessis' *Writing beyond the Ending: Narrative Strategies of Twentieth-Century
Women Writers* (Bloomington: Indiana University Press, 1985); and Jane Marcus, *Vir-
gina Woolf and the Languages of Patriarchy* (Bloomington: Indiana University Press,
1987).

[4]See Margaret Homans, *Bearing the Word: Language and Female Experience in
Nineteenth-Century Women's Writing* (Chicago: University of Chicago Press, 1986), especially pp. 1–39, for a feminist treatment of an alternative, "maternal" mode of
expression, which manages to appropriate the Lacanian account of cognitive and
linguistic development while avoiding the implication of silencing inherent in the
Kristevan premise of a semiotic order.

metaphor of an "other side" to a story purporting to be "the" story and that this figure was singularly fruitful for my own consideration of contemporary feminist narrative. Cliches tend to have unanticipated potency in relevant contexts, and certainly the notion of telling the other side of the story in many ways describes the enterprise of feminist criticism, perhaps even of feminist theorizing generally. Much of the power of the metaphor here derives from the fact that it makes visible the association of alterity—otherness—with woman as a social, cultural, and linguistic construction: Other *as* woman, or in Luce Irigaray's provocative conflation, the Other Woman. But the other side of the story is also, if implicitly, another story. The notion that stories inevitably both obscure and encode other stories has been axiomatic to our understanding of narrative since at least the eighteenth century; when construed as repressed or suppressed stories *of the Other*, these other stories become the enabling conditions for the writing and reading of feminist narrative.

I

Stories in the modern sense are always *somebody's* stories: even when they have a conventionally omniscient narrator they entail a point of view, take sides.[5] Such a perspectival notion of story implies that the coherence of one line of narration rests on the suppression of any number of "other sides," alternative versions that might give the same sequence of events an entirely different set of emphases and values. One immediate consequence is that even though conventions governing the selection of narrator, protagonist, and especially plot restrict the kinds of literary production that count as stories in a given society and historical period, changes in emphasis and value can articulate the "other side" of a culturally mandated story, exposing the limits it inscribes in the process of affirming a dominant ideology.

[5]Ian Watt observes that the rise of realism in the late eighteenth century denoted "a belief in the individual apprehension of reality through the senses"; because stories in these terms are ultimately grounded in individual apprehension, they entail a point or points of view even when they employ omniscient narrators. *The Rise of the Novel: Studies in Defoe, Richardson, and Fielding* (Berkeley: University of California Press, 1959), p. 14.

For example, in the eighteenth and nineteenth centuries, both male and female authors produced what Nancy Miller has termed "heroine's texts," novels with sexually vulnerable female protagonists whose entire futures turn on the possibility of being integrated into the surrounding society through a successful marriage.[6] As a number of feminist critics have recently demonstrated, many of the female writers during that period made it at least part of their project to articulate the "other side" of this story, stressing the constrictions of the romance plot and thus how this plot enforces the prevailing cultural construction of female identity and destiny.[7] Jane Austen foregrounded the economic necessity motivating marriage and, through the exemplary situations of her peripheral female characters, showed how likely it was that marriage would prove a painful necessity, psychologically damaging if not spiritually annihilating. Charlotte Brontë modified or withheld a narrative closure that her novels revealed inevitably to be an *en*closure, ultimately entrapping the heroine. George Eliot made a central theme of the female martyrdom inherent in both the "dysphoric" and the "euphoric" endings of the romance plot—that is, not only in those endings that resolved the situation created by the sexual susceptibility of the protagonist by terminating her life but in those endings that resolved the same situation by absorbing her into a conventionally happy marriage.[8] Indeed, one reason that "heroine's texts" written by women remained vital for so long and can still engage reader expectations may well be that in revealing the "other side" of an apparently simple and familiar story, female novelists imbedded a cultural critique that introduced complication and novelty.

[6]Nancy K. Miller, *The Heroine's Text: Reading in the French and English Novel, 1722–1782* (New York: Columbia University Press, 1980).

[7]Some of these readings now constitute cornerstones of the Anglo-American feminist tradition. Among the most important are Mary Jacobus, "The Buried Letter: *Villette*," and "Men of Maxims and *The Mill on the Floss*," both reprinted in her *Reading Women: Essays in Feminist Criticism* (New York: Columbia University Press, 1986), pp. 41–61 and pp. 62–79; Sandra M. Gilbert and Susan Gubar, *The Madwoman in the Attic: The Woman Writer and the Nineteenth-Century Literary Tradition* (New Haven: Yale University Press, 1979); and Elaine Showalter, *A Literature of Their Own: British Women Novelists from Brontë to Lessing* (Princeton: Princeton University Press, 1977).

[8]Miller, *The Heroine's Text*, p. xi.

The "other side" thus has a venerable history of being the woman's side, the version that discloses how the heroine is constrained by a set of narrative givens not of her own making. By the same token, however, it affirms woman's side as the side of an Other constructed by a maculinist discourse, as the place of an anterior femininity defined by reference to the masculine norm. As Simone de Beauvoir has observed, "woman" in these terms is a relational sign: "She is defined and differentiated with reference to man and not he with reference to her; she is the incidental, the inessential as opposed to the essential. He is the Subject, he is the Absolute—she is the Other."[9] The constraints that the female writer exposes and articulates are the constraints that define the position of "woman" within a system of linguistic oppositions. They guarantee that the female writer speaks from this position even as she denounces it.

Because this concept of woman as subordinate and supplementary Other was particularly involved in with the conventionally clear and unproblematic discourse of eighteenth- and nineteenth-century realism, many female fiction writers of the early twentieth century regarded themselves as having a vested interest in the modernist project of unsettling realist assumptions by overturning realist conventions. Rachel Blau DuPlessis has shown how stylistic and structural "ruptures" in works by writers as diverse as Olive Shreiner, Dorothy Richardson, Virginia Woolf, and H.D. constitute strategies to evade or undo an established system of representation that dictated the imaginable varieties of male and female possibility in the same gesture as it dictated the permissible varieties of narrative sequence, character, and relationship.[10] But to a great extent, these female attempts to write other-wise, to create an experimental syntax and structure that would not merely expose but would refuse altogether the prevailing constructions of gender and genre, were *read* back into the discourse they tried to challenge or circumvent. "Ruptures," after all, are easily integrated into the familiar account of femininity as inferiority or lack. Effects conceived as subversions of a literary tradition may be construed as failures to work within that

[9]Simone de Beauvoir, *The Second Sex* (New York: Bantam, 1961), p. xvi.
[10]See DuPlessis, *Writing beyond the Ending*, especially pp. 1–19 and pp. 31–46.

tradition, mimetically motivated by a limited female point of view or breadth of experience or, in more extreme accounts, by an inherently flawed female nature. The works of these writers were simply assimilated into literary history—or, more frequently, excised from literary history—as further evidence of woman's subordinate and supplementary otherness.

The dilemma that women writers encounter in their project of telling the other side of the story clearly has affinities with the debate over sexual difference currently preoccupying feminist theorists on both sides of the Atlantic.[11] On one hand, the woman writer is often working explicitly from the recognition that received notions of plot, character, sequence, and even the grammatical structures in which these notions are received presume a dichotomy of same/other that institutes and preserves sexual difference within a binary schema of dominant and muted values. On the other hand, her attempts to overthrow or evade the terms of her inherited tradition are liable to be co-opted by these same terms, so that resistance is reinscribed as the failure inherent in the very concept of feminine literary endeavor. The question of literary intention becomes embroiled in the question of literary re-

[11]The issue is probably the most fundamental and certainly the most controversial in feminist theory over the past ten years. On one hand, any privileging of the differences between subjects gendered masculine and subjects gendered feminine threatens to turn into wholesale acceptance of the cultural stereotypes that institute and maintain sexism. On the other hand, insisting on a *lack* of difference between masculine and feminine subjects threatens to assimilate everyone to a masculinist system of values—to what Luce Irigaray perceptively calls the economy of the Same. For perhaps the most far-reaching discussion of the suppression of difference in Western culture, see Irigaray, *Speculum of the Other Woman*, trans. Gillian C. Gill (Ithaca: Cornell University Press, 1985). Other key English-language documents in the dispute include Hester Eisenstein and Alice Jardine, eds., *The Future of Difference* (Boston: G. K. Hall, 1980); Elaine Marks and Isabelle de Courtivron, eds., *New French Feminisms* (Amherst: University of Massachusetts Press, 1980); Ann Rosalind Jones, "Writing the Body: Toward an Understanding of L'Ecriture Féminine," *Feminist Studies* 7 (Summer 1981), reprinted in Elaine Showalter, ed., *The New Feminist Criticism: Essays on Women, Literature, and Theory* (New York: Pantheon Books, 1985), pp. 361–77; Alice Jardine, *Gynesis: Configurations of Women and Modernity* (Ithaca: Cornell University Press, 1985); Toril Moi, *Sexual/Textual Politics: Feminist Literary Theory* (London: Methuen, 1985); Gayle Greene and Coppelia Kahn, eds., *Making a Difference: Feminist Literary Criticism* (London: Methuen, 1985); and Teresa de Lauretis, *Technologies of Gender: Essays on Theory, Film, and Fiction* (Bloomington: Indiana University Press, 1987).

ception, and in the process two meanings of otherness—otherness as a deliberate project of writing other-wise, and otherness as an unavoidable *effect* of a preexisting limit called femininity—seem almost inextricably conflated.

Far from being the discoveries of recent feminist theory, these issues of a gendered otherness and of how this otherness is construed by the surrounding culture are repeatedly raised within women's experimental writings in the twentieth century. For instance, in Dorothy Richardson's *Pilgrimage*, a thirteen-volume *Kunstlerroman* written largely between 1913 and 1938, the protagonist, Miriam Henderson, reflects that the stories she is trying to write are not, like her best work, "alive all over"; she locates the paradoxical source of her problem in a man's encouragement and in the expectations this encouragement tacitly raises:

> It was Bob, driving so long ago a little nail into her mind when he said, "Write the confessions of a modern woman," meaning a sensational chronicle with an eye, several eyes, upon the interest of sympathetic readers like himself—"Woman, life's heroine, the dear, exasperating creature"—who really likes to see how life looks from the other side, the woman's side, who put me on the wrong track and created all those lifeless pages. Following them up, everything would be left out that is always there, preceding and accompanying and surviving the drama of human relationships; the reality from which people move away as soon as they closely approach and expect each other to be all in all.[12]

Although this passage begins from the identification of "the other side" with "the woman's side," it does so only to reject this identification as dictated by masculine desire, by a voyeurism frankly prurient in its assumption that this side will reveal itself in the form of "confessions," a "sensational chronicle" presumed by the man who solicits it to be intended for "sympathetic readers like himself." Otherness becomes the thing disclosed by the glimpse into the seraglio, the posited subjectivity that emerges only as the *object* of male scrutiny. It is accessory to the dominant sensibility, lovably "exasperating" in its subordination and consequent irrationality. Miriam here acknowledges that this supposi-

[12]Dorothy Richardson, *Dimple Hill*, vol. 4 of *Pilgrimage*, (New York: Alfred A. Knopf, 1967), p. 525.

tion of an otherness brought into being by the requirements of a male audience has put her on the "wrong track," leading her to create "lifeless pages." The characteristic pronominal slide in the opening sentence of this passage—from the third-person "her mind" to the first-person "put me on the wrong track"—suggests how such provocation throws Miriam into the position of a speaking subjectivity, inasmuch as she cannot at the moment of realization go on occupying what she recognizes as a voyeur's stance on female experience.

Yet *Pilgrimage* has traditionally been *read* as if it constituted the "confessions of a modern woman": as if its stylistic innovations, including the "stream of consciousness" narrative mode that it pioneered, resulted from a sort of authorial striptease, whereby self-exposure spontaneously generated its own discourse. A contemporary critic compared it to "the collections of a lifetime, a boxful of scraps of old silk and stuff such as hoarding women gather and leave behind at death," and the gendered character of the assemblage he describes ("hoarding women" appear to gather without taxonomizing and perhaps even without examining) engenders questions about advertency, about "whether . . . such impressionism [is] anything more than a marvellous feat of memory, of reproduction," and about "how far deliberate is that portrait [of Miriam]? Is it not there, inferentially, as it were, by the accumulated indications? How far is the character *created*?"[13] If *Pilgrimage* was widely conceded to be the first major work of the twentieth century to present "the other side, the woman's side," it was also trivialized by that concession, becoming simply the imprint of "life's heroine" as she flung herself onto the page.

In the quoted passage from the novel, however, Miriam explicitly rejects the version of her enterprise that equates women's writing with "confessions" and goes on to provide what amounts to a negative manifesto for the project of *Pilgrimage* itself—by implication, the book she will be able to write when she transcends the demands that have produced "lifeless pages." The project is one of inclusion and involves changing the principles of selection that have governed

[13]Frank Swinnerton, *The Georgian Scene* (New York: Farrar and Rinehart, 1934), pp. 386–87.

the kind of novel in which "woman" figures as "life's heroine." What Miriam proposes is to bring into her fiction the events "preceding and accompanying and surviving the drama of human relationships"—that is, to honor the continuity of lived experience, replacing the realist representation of "key" events in causal sequence with a mode of representation that she regards as closer to the configurations of reality.[14] The enterprise is strikingly similar to Virginia Woolf's famous formulation: "Life is not a series of gig-lamps symmetrically arranged; life is a luminous halo, a semi-transparent envelope surrounding us from the beginning of consciousness to the end. Is it not the task of the novelist to convey this varying, this unknown and uncircumscribed spirit, whatever aberration or complexity it may display, with as little mixture of the alien and external as possible?"[15] But while Woolf's attack on realism is couched in strategically general terms, in that the thing in need of accurate depiction is that large entity "life," Richardson's emphasis is on representations of female experience and thus on the question of whether a *woman's* life is accurately rendered as a selection of incidents "symmetrically arranged," specifically, as a selection of those incidents involving women in "the drama of human relationships" in which the members of a heterosexual couple "expect each other to be all in all." The realism that Miriam Henderson finds "lifeless" is precisely the heroine's text. The project that Richardson delineates for her writer-protagonist at once honors the modernist demand for fidelity to the continuum that is conscious experience and writes the quondam heroine out of the constrictions of her cultural text by using the model of the continuum to undo selection and priority: in particular, the selection of events leading up to and culminating in a marriage and the priority placed on this romance plot as the sole meaning of female experience. The narrative mode of *Pilgrimage* celebrated in May Sinclair's famous description—

[14]The implied judgment—that realism fails to be realistic *enough*—was a modernist commonplace: Virginia Woolf castigated Arnold Bennett for concentrating so much on details of housing, apparel, and economy that he failed to depict that exemplar of "human character" Mrs Brown "as she is," for instance. See "Mr Bennett and Mrs Brown" in Woolf, *The Captain's Death Bed and Other Essays* (London: Hogarth Press, 1950), pp. 99–111.

[15]Virginia Woolf, "Modern Fiction" in Virginia Woolf, *Collected Essays* (London: Hogarth Press, 1966), 2:106.

"There is no drama, no situation, no set scene. Nothing happens. It is just life going on and on. It is Miriam Henderson's stream of consciousness going on and on"[16]—is also the vehicle whereby Miriam herself goes on and on, passing through the various enclosures that contained and summed up her eighteenth- and nineteenth-century predecessors: the nurseries and schoolrooms; the ballrooms, chapels, music rooms, and walled gardens; the kitchens and bedrooms of married friends and relatives; and most significant, the gentlemen's rooms, and even the gentlemen's arms. If in thirteen volumes Miriam manages to slip through any number of potentially entrapping social situations that threaten to terminate her story by marrying her off or disgracing her to the point where suicide becomes her only option, she also exists within a narrative structure that dissolves much of the teleology of the romance plot by supplanting the realist emphasis on event and sequence with a characteristically modernist emphasis on the indivisibility of consciousness, and thus on continuity.[17]

II

The project of writing another *kind* of story in effect enables Richardson to present "the other side, the woman's side" without accepting a maculinist definition of what this "side" consists of. Her example suggests how the literary movements of the twentieth century that arose in opposition to realism—most evidently modernism and postmodernism—have strong affinities with a specifically feminist interrogation of the assumptions encoded in realist conventions. Yet despite these affinities, there are fewer female writers in the canons of twentieth-century narrative experiment than in the canon of English nineteenth-century realism.

The point is so obvious that it rarely provokes comment. Any list

[16]May Sinclair, "The Novels of Dorothy Richardson," *Egoist* 5 (April 1918), 57–68.
[17]For an illuminating discussion of the connections between Richardson's feminism and modernism, see especially Sydney Janet Kaplan, *Feminine Consciousness in the Modern British Novel* (Urbana: University of Illinois Press, 1975), pp. 8–46. For a description of the main formal characteristics of realism and modernism, see David Lodge, *The Modes of Modern Writing: Metaphor, Metonymy, and the Typology of Modern Literature* (Ithaca: Cornell University Press, 1977), especially pp. 25–27 and pp. 45–47.

of great English novelists in the nineteenth century (the sort of list that determines examination subjects for graduate students in English, for instance, and that also lurks, if less visibly, behind the decisions about course offerings made by the academic departments in which they are enrolled) is almost certain to contain Jane Austen, one or two Brontës, and George Eliot.[18] In the twentieth century, even when national boundaries fade away in the canon makers' acknowledgment of an International Modernism, only one woman, Virginia Woolf, finds a place in the company of Joyce, Conrad, Lawrence, Forster, Ford, Fitzgerald, Hemingway, and Faulkner.[19] The postmodernist canon, similarly international, is even more rigorously masculinist. In an essay surveying recent literature sufficiently innovative and interesting to warrant being called postmodern, John Barth mentions no woman writing in English; and indeed only one woman, Nathalie Sarraute, appears on Barth's list, although there are twenty-three men, among them William Gass, John Hawkes, Donald Barthelme, Robert Coover, Stanley Elkin, Thomas Pynchon, Kurt Vonnegut, Vladimir Nabokov, John Fowles, and Barth himself.[20]

[18]The nineteenth-century American canon, however, is wholly male, largely because female writers were working in a separate—and thus detachable—genre. For an examination of the sentimental novel and its disappearance from American literary histories, see Jane P. Tompkins, *Sensational Designs: The Cultural Work of American Fiction, 1790–1860* (New York: Oxford University Press, 1985).

[19]Hugh Kenner's essay "The Making of the Modernist Canon" (in *Canons*, ed. Robert von Hallberg [Chicago: University of Chicago Press, 1984], p. 371) relegates her to secondary status as "not part of International Modernism; she is an English novelist of manners, writing village gossip from a village called Bloomsbury for her English readers."

[20]John Barth, "The Literature of Replenishment," in John Barth, *The Friday Book: Essays and Other Nonfiction* (New York: G. P. Putnam's Sons, 1984), pp. 193–206. Larry McCaffery's compendious *Postmodern Fiction: A Bio-bibliographical Guide* (Westport, Conn.: Greenwood, 1986), extends the boundaries of the genre to include such neorealists as Raymond Carver and Ann Beattie as well as such disparate writers of nonfictional theory and criticism as Harold Bloom, Paul de Man, Jerome Klinkowitz, Jacques Derrida, and Michel Foucault (the practitioners of *écriture féminine* are conspicuously absent from this assembly) and still comes up with only eleven women as opposed to ninety-five men. It is also interesting that the "guide" section passes over most of the forty-two authors discussed in Bonnie Zimmerman's article "Feminist Fiction and the Postmodern Challenge," which is included in the "overview" section, pp. 175–88. To be sure, Zimmerman contends that despite "a demonstratively reflexive, experimental tendency in some feminist fiction," there are nevertheless

The judgment both assumed and fostered by such catalogues is that women are conservative, upholders of tradition and thus to be found among the perpetuators of a realism that continues to flourish alongside the modes of writing that play off it. Reasons have even been advanced for this presumptive state of affairs— for example, that women have "too much to say" to fool around with structural niceties. But such justifications regard realist form as transparent in the service of content and thus make precisely the assumption that both modernism and postmodernism dispute: that realism is something like a "natural" or "straight" mode of writing that does not involve stylistic choices in the way that experimental writing does.

Rather ironically, the notion that women are in this sense "natural" or "straight" writers, who manage to get reality—particularly their own experiences—onto the page with a minimum of art or decision making, has informed a whole practice of feminist criticism, so that some of the most important examples of this criticism have fostered the association between women's writing and aesthetic conservatism. Many of the Anglo-American feminist critics who began with the intent of doing justice to women's fiction as a chronicle of female experience seem to have found themselves in the process purveying an exaggerated theory of mimesis, in which authors are simply mirrored in their own texts.[21] This tendency led on a more sophisticated level to developments like the Sandra Gilbert and Susan Gubar "anxiety of authorship" paradigm of women's writing, in which realist conventions of sequence, plot, and character are assumed as norms, and all deviations are attributed to unrecognized

---

"relatively few examples of truly postmodernist feminist novels" (pp. 176–77). But on the other hand, relatively few of the ninety-five male authors represented would qualify as "truly postmodernist" by the criteria Zimmerman adduces. Nor do her criteria explain such editorial choices as William Kennedy but not Grace Paley or Jacques Derrida but not Hélène Cixous.

[21]Some of the most important documents for the development of the discipline Elaine Showalter calls gynocriticism—critical approaches to writing by women—have this limitation, including Showalter's own book *A Literature of Their Own* and Ellen Moers's *Literary Women* (New York: Doubleday, 1976). I should add, however, that the presumption of autobiography proves less of a problem in these two works than in some of the (less careful and self-conscious) studies they have engendered.

eruptions of repressed biographical material acting as *dis*ruptions of an otherwise traditional text.[22] Both the biographically mimetic and the "anxiety of authorship" models involve what Mary Jacobus has identified as "an unstated complicity with the autobiographical 'phallacy,' whereby male critics hold that women's writing is somehow closer to [women's] experience than men's, that the female text *is* the author, or at any rate a dramatic extension of her unconsciousness."[23] As a consequence, both of these models tend to elide the distinction between the woman writer's deliberate attempts to create innovative and disruptive narrative structures or styles—to write other-wise—and the otherness that a masculinist culture posits and expects of "woman, life's heroine, the dear exasperating creature." When women writers emerge as "different," this difference tends to be attributed to their perspective, to their situation in society, to their temperament, or in the most extreme cases to their nature. It is rarely, and only in passing, attributed to their conscious agency.

In the contemporary period, and especially for the body of fiction written after 1960, "women's writing" is a category almost completely outside the dominant experimental movement of postmodernism. The prevailing assumption seems to be that female writers are interested in "other things" than formal experimentation: in psychological subtleties, personal relationships, social accommodation, or revolution.[24] Once again, this model presumes a "natural"

---

[22]Gilbert and Gubar, *The Madwoman in the Attic*, pp. 45–91. The strengths of this extremely important book lie in its meticulous and ambitious close readings, and as in the case of Showalter and Moers, the problems arise less in the parent work than in the less canny and sophisticated studies it influenced.

[23]Mary Jacobus, review of *The Madwoman in the Attic* in *Signs: A Journal of Women in Culture and Society* 6, no. 3 (1981), 520.

[24]Ann Barr Snitow notes, "Feminism and postmodernism have largely ignored each other, perhaps to the detriment of both," but she advances an important political reason for the concentration of feminist criticism on feminine realism: "The realist novel has always been the novel of such first phases [as the contemporary resurgence of feminist consciousness]. Since the inception of the form, novels have been 'how-to' manuals for groups gathering their identity through self-description." See "The Front Line: Notes on Sex in Novels by Women, 1969–1979," *Signs: A Journal of Women in Culture and Society* 5, no. 5 (1980), 705. Bonnie Zimmerman observes, "We might expect that a feminist literary program would demand the rejection of realism as inherently male-defined," but adds that feminist writers have largely avoided postmodernism because it is historically a masculinist genre, incorporating sexual stereo-

or "straight" style and structure subordinate to and in service of content. Even when such presumptions intend to value "having something to say" over the stylistic and structural modes that mediate the "saying," they consign women to subordinate roles in literary culture inasmuch as they consign women writers to the conservation of past traditions. In any period of literary history, new and innovative writing tends to supersede writing that maintains and continues older practices: canonization is, among other things, a means of consolidating the emblematic forms with which the period comes to be identified. As David Lodge has noted, realism never stopped being a vital movement, insofar as vitality is measured in the number and popularity of realist writers.[25] But despite the number and popularity of realist writers between 1900 and 1945, the canonized works of the modern period are the works of "high" modernism, just as the likely-to-be-canonized or "precanonized" works of the contemporary period are for the most part works of postmodernism.[26] The writing perceived as the avant-garde at a par-

---

types and privileging depictions of sexual violence, and because "feminists shared the commonplace perception of this fiction as the literature of alienation and exhaustion" ("Feminist Fiction and the Postmodern Challenge," p. 176). See also Joanne S. Frye, *Living Stories, Telling Lives: Women and the Novel in Contemporary Experience* (Ann Arbor: University of Michigan Press, 1986), especially pp. 37–38.

[25]In *The Modes of Modern Writing*, Lodge makes an impressive case for the importance of realist writing among English novelists in the modern period, citing Woolf's nemeses Arnold Bennett, H. G. Wells, and John Galsworthy, along with subsequent generations beginning with George Orwell, Christopher Isherwood, and Graham Greene, and followed by Angus Wilson, C. P. Snow, Kingsley Amis, Anthony Powell, Alan Sillitoe, and Margaret Drabble (he might also have added David Lodge). But his admission that "we have no term for the kind of modern fiction that is not modernist except 'realistic' (sometimes qualified by 'traditionally' or 'conventionally' or 'social')" betrays that even important fiction of this sort stays outside a canon that makes moder*nism* the defining feature of the modern period.

[26]See Richard Ohmann, "The Shaping of a Canon: U.S. Fiction, 1960–1975," in *Canons*, ed. von Hallberg, pp. 377–401. Ohmann places illuminating emphasis on the material conditions of contemporary canonization—agents, publishers, reviews, and advertisements in reviewing journals—and not surprisingly, his emergent American "precanon" turns out to be disproportionately masculine. For example, the *Wilson Quarterly*'s "1977 or 1978" poll of professors of American literature yielded a list of eleven novels judged to be "most important" in post–1960 American writing; all are by men (p. 384). A list from *Contemporary Literary Criticism* constituting, in Ohmann's view, "a sampling of the interests of those who set literary standards," yields seven women and forty-one men, admittedly a better ratio than McCaffery's more recent bio-bibliography of postmodern fiction. But despite his therapeutic cynicism about

ticular moment tends to define that moment in literary history. Other practices elicit at best a contextual footnote as indexes of the popular or mass culture of the time; at worst, the record ignores them entirely.

But while much American feminist criticism has concentrated on the woman who writes and the female experience represented, in the process presuming a realist or even a confessional mode of women's fiction, another strain of feminist criticism has demonstrated that the decentering and destabilizing tendencies of recent experimental writing have a great deal in common with the feminist project of overturning culturally constructed oppositions, among them the oppositions that constitute the powerful codes of gender. Aligning literary postmodernism with poststructuralist theory and the *écriture féminine* of such writers as Luce Irigaray and Hélène Cixous, Alice Jardine celebrates all three practices as manifestations of an alternative discourse aiming to "give a new language to these other spaces" that are subordinated in the traditional Western dichotomies: body rather than mind, nature rather than culture, other rather than same, woman rather than man.[27] Theorists of postmodernism on both sides of the Atlantic similarly affirm that their movement shares a political agenda with feminism, inasmuch as to destabilize narrative relations between dominant and subordinate, container and contained, is also to destabilize the social and cultural relations of dominance and containment by which the conventionally masculine subsumes and envelops the conventionally feminine.[28] Because feminism has a stake in the undoing of hierarchy and containment, it appears that writing commonly described in terms of its subversive newness, as avant-garde or postmodern, can also

---

the "greatness" identified or instilled by canonization, Ohmann never remarks on the gender bias of his findings.

[27]Jardine, *Gynesis*, pp. 72–73.

[28]See, for example, Jean François Lyotard, "One of the Things at Stake in Women's Struggles," *Sub-Stance* 20 (1978), 9–17; and Craig Owens, "The Discourse of Others: Feminists and Postmodernism," in *The Anti-Aesthetic: Essays on Postmodern Culture*, ed. Hal Foster (Port Townsend, Wash.: Bay Press, 1983), pp. 57–82. For a more disaffected appraisal, see Nancy Fraser and Linda J. Nicholson, "Social Criticism without Philosophy: An Encounter between Feminism and Postmodernism," *Communication* 10 (1988), 345–66.

be described in terms of its subversive political implications, as "feminine" or feminist writing.

There is, however, an irony attendant on this identification, which is poignantly illustrated by Linda Hutcheon in a review article that addresses the overlapping concerns of recent metafiction and recent feminist theory. Hutcheon characterizes metafiction by its "subversion of the stability of point of view" and aligns this "subversion" with the disintegration of the bourgeois, patriarchal subject. But the books that she chooses to illustrate this point are all by men, and as a consequence her argument tends to imply that feminism is so purely a product of literary language that it is entirely restricted to the domain of literary representation. To be sure, her topic is precisely "the relation of non-coincidence between the discursive construct of 'woman' and the historical subjects called 'women,' " but the "historical subjects called 'women' " with whom she in fact deals are discursive constructs produced by male authors. In effect, her whole discussion is framed by the premise of male authority.[29]

To give the problem its most radical formulation, it would seem that in the contemporary period, fictional experimentation has everything to do with feminism and nothing to do with women—and emphatically nothing to do with women as points of origin, as authors. Yet alongside the theoretical writing that appears to set up this disjunction, there exist a number of structurally and stylistically interesting fictional works by female authors, works that might well be regarded as experimental if it were possible to discount the reviews and criticism that, with ingenuity and even sympathy, trans-

[29]Linda Hutcheon, "Subject in/of/to History and His Story," *Diacritics* 16, no. 1 (Spring 1986), 80, 83. Similarly, in the early work of Hélène Cixous the two great "feminine writers" are Jean Genet and James Joyce. See Cixous, *The Exile of James Joyce; or, The Art of Replacement*, trans. Sally Purcell (New York: David Lewis, 1972). Alice Jardine notes Cixous's focus on Genet, Hölderlin, Kafka, Kleist, Shakespeare, Derrida, Heidegger, Kierkegaard, and Lacan and glosses, "Because in the past women have always written 'as men,' Cixous hardly ever alludes to women writers" (*Gynesis*, p. 62). Here, as in the case of Hutcheon's discussion, it may be worth wondering about the political efficacy of writing "as women" or of textual feminism if the practice is restricted almost entirely to men—and to luminaries of the literary and philosophical canon at that.

late experimentalism into flawed realism (for example, faulting a utopian romance for being insufficiently plausible) or into hyperbolic mimesis (for example, presuming that a disjointed narrative reflects the state of mind of a flaky or insane heroine). My own enterprise here might be to indicate an "other side" to these critical accounts, specifically to indicate ways in which works by Rhys, Lessing, Walker, and Atwood have eluded or overflowed certain established modes of reading and ways in which we might learn to read—as they write—other-wise.[30]

[30]Nancy Miller's important essay "Arachnologies: The Woman, the Text, and the Critic," in *The Poetics of Gender*, ed. Miller (New York: Columbia University Press, 1986), pp. 270–95, calls for a strategy of *overreading* women's writing that seems fundamentally akin to my own demand—and practice.

Chapter 1
Writing in the Margins: Jean Rhys

One of the most striking aspects of the current Jean Rhys revival is the extent to which readers united in their determination to praise Rhys have divided on the issue of autobiography in her novels. The mainstream critics who undertook the rehabilitation of her reputation in the early 1970s seemed to find the autobiographical sources of her subject matter a distraction, if not an outright embarrassment.[1] They were inclined instead to stress the formal finish and control of her prose style, to admire her ironic distance from the characters and incidents she describes, and to universalize her protagonists and the situations in which they find themselves, to the point where Rhys was represented as writing, as Elgin Mellown puts it, about "woman in one of her archetypal roles." Diana Trilling goes further:

[1]Rhys published one collection of short stories and four novels between 1927 and 1939, after which she effectively disappeared from public notice until 1956, when the actress Selma Vaz Dias (who had actually been in contact with Rhys, with interruptions, since 1949) had the BBC place an advertisement in the *New Statesman*. "Rediscovered" by this maneuver, Rhys felt encouraged to write the novel *Wide Sargasso Sea* (1966) and to publish two more collections of stories and an "unfinished autobiography" before her death in 1979. The appearance of *Wide Sargasso Sea* resuscitated her reputation and led to the reissuing of the earlier novels. A. Alvarez's review essay, "The Best Living English Novelist" (*New York Times Book Review*, 17 March 1974, 6–7) and Howard Moss's "Going to Pieces" in the "Books" column of the *New Yorker* (50 [16 December 1974], 161–62) are two of the key critical pieces establishing Rhys as a major, indeed a canonical English writer. Judith Thurman's article "The Mistress and the Mask: Jean Rhys's Fiction" (*MS* 4 [January 1976], 51–52, 91) was one of the first major documents for feminist readings of Rhys's work.

Rhys is not writing about "woman" at all and certainly not about "the plight of the sensitive woman." The novels "are far from being exercises in female literary narcissism; she deals with something more palpable, the hard terror of psychological isolation."[2]

On the other hand, and certainly in reaction to readings that eschewed "female literary narcissism" to the point of either turning Rhys's protagonists into sexless emblems or regarding them as the unsavory subjects of quasi-scientific study,[3] the feminist critics who addressed Rhys's writings tended to emphasize that Rhys herself bears a strong resemblance to all her main characters and has undergone experiences similar to events chronicled in all her novels. As biographical material became more available, such critics increasingly treated the historical Jean Rhys as a gloss on her own characters. As a consequence, they regularly conflated creator and creation in the interests of discerning motives for both. Teresa O'Connor is representative: "Certainly boredom and domination figure in Rhys's work as themes but they are symptoms and results of a deeper malaise: the dislocation and alienation that comes from having neither a true home, metaphorically and literally, nor a loving mother, which for many may be the equivalent—and no way of fabricating either. It was Rhys's mother's indifference to her which forced Rhys to become indifferent in return. It is her heroines' statelessness, homelessness and lack of familial and deep ties that lead to their malaise."[4] O'Connor initially identifies boredom and dom-

---

[2]Elgin W. Mellown, "Characters and Themes in the Novels of Jean Rhys," in *Contemporary Women Novelists*, ed. Patricia Meyer Spacks (Englewood Cliffs, N.J.: Prentice-Hall, 1977), p. 123; Diana Trilling, "The Liberated Heroine," *Times Literary Supplement*, 13 October 1978, 1164. See also A. Alvarez, "The Best Living English Novelist," which admires the "unblinking truthfulness" of the novels but minimizes their political implications in New Critical terms and thus, inadvertently, trivializes Rhys's political intelligence: she "is absolutely nonintellectual: no axe to grind, no ideas to tout" (p. 7).

[3]For example, Peter Wolfe cites as Rhys's "main contribution to modern literature a shrewd yet sympathetic look . . . at a character type heretofore ignored, patronized, or used merely to flesh out a social category—the dispossessed urban spinster. No liberal-humanist heroine, the archetypal Rhys figure lacks ideas, job, and man" (Introduction *Jean Rhys* [Boston: Twayne/G. K. Hall, 1980], n.p.). In a letter to Francis Wyndham, Rhys recalls a less ambiguous appraisal of one of her novels in the same terms—this a rejection of *Good Morning, Midnight* (dated 14 May 1964, *Letters*, p. 277): " 'This is not a novel but a case history' or something like that."

[4]Teresa F. O'Connor, *Jean Rhys: The West Indian Novels* (New York: New York University Press, 1986), p. 35.

ination as "symptoms" without explaining whose symptoms they are, so that the ensuing discussion of homelessness and motherlessness suggests that the "deeper malaise" may afflict society as a whole. But the discussion then shifts from the implicitly political to the explicitly personal and psychological—"It was Rhys's mother's indifference to her which forced Rhys to become indifferent in return"—and with no other connective than parallelism, shifts again, this time to the protagonists of Rhys's fiction—"It is her heroines' statelessness, homelessness and lack of familial and deep ties that lead to their malaise." Rhys's own "deeper malaise" is assumed to produce heroines suffering from the same malaise. And despite the meticulousness of O'Connor's study in other matters, notably the quotation and citation of manuscript material, it assumes without any discussion of the subject that Rhys was unaware of her own motivation for creating such women and consequently of the motivation that presumably provoked these women into acting the way she caused them to act.

Rhys herself complained about this sort of fuzzing of the distinction between author and character. In a letter to her daughter Maryvonne Moerman, 22 June 1960, she writes:

> You know, I would like to send you a very short story and implore you to type it for me.
> It is not (repeat *not*) autobiography, and not to be taken seriously. But the people here are terribly narrow minded and they gossip like crazy.
> Really—this is true! I found it out in Bude I assure you. For them "I" is "I" and not a literary device. Every *word* is autobiography![5]

Apparently her complaint applies to readers more sophisticated than her neighbors in rural Cornwall.[6] If mainstream critics have insisted on her irony and control at the expense of the characters thus distanced and manipulated (as when Peter Wolfe applauds her for having performed "the rare feat of writing good books

---

[5]Francis Wyndham and Diana Melly, eds., *The Letters of Jean Rhys* (New York: Viking/Elizabeth Sifton Books, 1984), p. 187. The story in question, "Let Them Call It Jazz," was in fact based on some of Rhys's experiences in the women's prison at Halloway. For an account of the series of bizarre incidents leading to Rhys's imprisonment, see *Letters*, pp. 57, 76.

[6]Carole Angier, *Jean Rhys* (New York: Viking, 1985), unabashedly reads the novels and stories as if they were "confessions" of the author and attributes comments by characters to the Rhys who is the same age at a similar stage in her life.

about dull characters trapped in numbing routines"),[7] many feminist critics have salvaged these characters by identifying them with the author, and in the process have turned Rhys's writing into compulsive self-revelation, a by-product of therapy. Rhys does tell her own story, of course, and in this respect she resembles many other twentieth-century writers. But to make biography the principle that governs interpretation of her works is to make Rhys unable to control the form and the ideology of her own text. There can be little question of innovation or even of technique, and no question of a deliberate challenge to the value presuppositions of the dominant culture, when criticism tries to naturalize the unsettling questions raised within a body of fiction by making them the effects of a constricted point of view that the author herself was unable to transcend.[8]

The unsettling questions raised within Rhys's fiction have overwhelmingly to do with character, particularly with the status of female protagonists whose social situations are strikingly similar throughout five novels, despite differences in age, background, and historical context. The shorthand term "Rhys woman" often designates this whole species of protagonist, and the "Rhys woman" remains the factor within Rhys's writing that has polarized the positive criticism, and the reason why other readers, many of them feminist, are hostile to Rhys's fiction.[9]

[7]Wolfe, Introduction to *Jean Rhys*, n.p.

[8]In this respect, Marsha Z. Cummins's accolade is representative of how even enthusiastic praise can damn. Cummins concludes her essay "Point of View in the Novels of Jean Rhys: The Effect of a Double Focus" (*World Literature Written in English* 24, [Autumn 1984]) with the observation, "Though Rhys could not imagine a new role for women beyond victimization, she could, at least, actively imagine the dead end of the old one" (371). Of this reflexive recourse to such "explanatory" principles as failure of imagination, Judith Kegan Gardiner comments, "When a writer like Joyce or Eliot writes about an alienated man estranged from himself, he is read as a portrait of the diminished possibilities of human existence in modern society. When Rhys writes about an alienated woman estranged from herself, critics applaud her perceptive but narrow depiction of female experience and tend to narrow her vision even further by labeling it both pathological and autobiographical" ("Good Morning, Midnight; Good Night, Modernism," *boundary two* 11 [Fall/Winter 1982–83], 247).

[9]Diane McPherson reminds me that the term "Rhys woman" tends to erase important differences between these characters and so to reinforce the implication that the novels are "mere" autobiography. I take her warning to heart: Rhys in no way wrote five novels about the *same* woman; she did write about five women in analogous situations.

I

The defining characteristic of the Rhys woman is her financial dependency on a man or, if she is well on her way down the road to economic and social devastation that Rhys's writing persistently maps, on men. She is sometimes employed as mannequin, artist's model, or chorus girl, sometimes delicately "unemployed"; various degrees of euphemism term her adventuress, mistress, or prostitute; other characters call her tart, *grue, petite femme,* or girl. No one calls her wife, although she sometimes is one: her dependency is inherently unrespectable.

In fact, what to call this protagonist is part of the problem of her status within the value systems of Rhys's fictional universes. Certainly the available names have a powerful ideological charge: in a class of mine that was reading *Voyage in the Dark,* one young man remarked wonderingly that he wasn't sure why we were taking a floozy so seriously. Less obviously, these names tend to obscure the situation in which the Rhys woman finds herself, as Arnold Davidson inadvertently demonstrates in trying to address what he sees as "contradictions" within the character of Julia Martin in *After Leaving Mr Mackenzie*: "Is she a woman selling herself to a limited clientele and for no set price, or is she a woman too ready to fall in love with some man from whom she can then accept assistance because financial gifts are tokens of his love for her? Is she essentially a mercenary or essentially a romantic? The answer, of course, is that she must be both and neither."[10] The "answer" proposed by Davidson renders a very common state of affairs paradoxical, largely because his presentation is conditioned by the assumption that a woman must be "essentially" either prostitute or beloved[11]—which is to say, either financially or emotionally dependent, but not both. The division here is the familiar one between stereotypically good and bad women, and Davidson's restatement of it is particularly helpful in revealing the contradictions inherent not in the situation of being

[10] Arnold E. Davidson, "The Art and Economics of Destitution in Jean Rhys's *After Leaving Mr Mackenzie*," *Studies in the Novel* 16 (Summer 1984), 217.

[11] Interestingly, the word that would evoke agency here, "lover," cannot be unambiguously applied to a woman in our society; we have no word to designate a woman emotionally involved with a man.

"both and neither" but in the division itself. A good woman is one who needs a man emotionally. Although she may also need his economic support to survive, this need must remain secondary, contingent, accidental; she is "essentially a romantic." On the other hand, a bad woman is one who needs—and cold-bloodedly uses— a man financially. Any demonstration of emotional commitment to this man is necessarily a manifestation of bad faith, or as Davidson puts it later, a "sustained pretense";[12] she is "essentially a mercenary." Of course, the historical condition of women has been to be "both and neither," which is only to say that these mutually exclusive designations do not accurately describe an ordinary situation.

Yet many readers find it difficult to call the situation of any of Rhys's protagonists ordinary, at least in part because the problems involved in naming these characters tend to invoke weirder problems about what to *do* with them, deposited as they are in the foreground of narratives that chronicle only their incapacity to control their own lives. The question of what to do with them arises because the Rhys woman doesn't seem to do much for herself, or not anything that works, nothing that significantly improves her situation or even renders it tragic. She is often characterized as "passive" or "masochistic" because her actions do not substantially change her lot, as if she did not have the *efficacy* to be a protagonist. And readers like the student who resented paying attention to a "floozy" tend to feel that if she is going to be this sort of person she ought to get out of the way, out of the spotlight; she ought to fade back into the shadows at the periphery of the story where they won't have to look at her all the time.

This last sort of reaction is valuable, precisely because it acknowledges how unsettling the Rhys woman is to dominant cultural presuppositions. Both mainstream and feminist critics who admire Rhys's fiction in effect try to settle her, accommodating her to these presuppositions either by interpreting her as an alien and inferior sort of person who serves as an object of study (in the process sacrificing authorial empathy), or by interpreting her as Rhys's own unexamined self-projection (in the process sacrificing authorial control). But such adjustments, made in order to justify the protagonist,

¹²Davidson, "Art and Economics," p. 218.

take for granted that the protagonist requires justification. They begin from the presumption that she is the sort of character who, under normal circumstances would not be major, and then they redefine the circumstances without questioning the underlying premises: that there are intrinsically major and minor characters, regardless of narrative context, and that certain categories of socially marginal human beings are by virtue of this social marginality fitted only to be minor characters.

To articulate these premises is to allow Jean Rhys's achievement to be restated in terms of radical innovation. Rhys continually places a marginal character at the center of her fiction and in doing so decenters an inherited narrative structure and undermines the values informing this structure.[13] In particular the novel, a form that emerged with the bourgeoisie and embodies the ethical priorities of this ascendant class, privileges agency—and, more insidiously, privileges the assumption that an agent who is motivated and tenacious enough will necessarily bring about the desired results. In his classic 1927 study *Aspects of the Novel*, E. M. Forster approvingly quotes the French critic Alain on the defining quality of the genre: "There is no fatality in the novel; there, everything is founded on human nature, and the dominating feeling is of an existence where everything is intentional, even passions and crimes, even misery." Forster goes on to use this observation only insofar as it supports his contention that "people in a novel can be understood completely by the reader, if the novelist wishes; their inner as well as their outer life can be exposed,"[14] but Alain's point is more far-reaching, if less obvious. The absence of fatality in the novel is translated into a "feeling" that "everything is intentional" and thus becomes the unarticulated basis for a philosophy of extreme voluntarism. In effect, Alain has exposed the convention that major characters in novels *bring things on themselves*, whether for good or ill. Except in certain marked and delimited cases, they are presumed to be free to stand,

[13]Philip Brian Harper makes this point about such writers as Djuna Barnes, Anaïs Nin, Nathanael West, and Ralph Ellison in "The Re-Centered Subject: Marginality in the Development of the Postmodernist Novel" (Ph.D. diss., Cornell University, 1988).

[14]E. M. Forster, *Aspects of the Novel* (1927; rpt. New York: Harcourt Brace Jovanovich, 1955), pp. 46, 47.

free to fall, which is to say capable of thinking and acting independently of most external and all internal constraints.[15]

In other words, major characters have free will, a power construed
by the bourgeois ideology informing the novel as the ability to
triumph over various kinds of obstacles—certainly over the intan-
gible obstacles erected within the mind by upbringing and received
opinion. Forster in effect recognizes this hyperbolic concept of autonomy when he makes unpredictability the distinguishing feature
of the "round" characters who in his opinion are protagonists of all
truly great novels: "The test of a round character is whether it is
capable of surprising in a convincing way."[16] But clearly not all
characters in a novel need to possess this sort of free will. Indeed,
certain of them can best support and contrast with major characters
by virtue of not having it, are convincing inasmuch as they are
*in*capable of surprising. These are what Forster terms "flat" characters; they are what they are, he maintains, to the point where they
can be summed up in a single sentence. Or even a single word.
They can often be assigned their permanent place in the fictional
universe simply by being assigned a name.

The concern to find a name for Rhys's protagonists is of course a
concern to place them in this definitive manner. The Rhys woman
is disorienting because names like "prostitute," "discarded mistress," and the anachronistic but heartfelt "floozy" do not suffice to
dismiss her from further consideration. Completely constrained
within a narrow social role, she yet possesses a centrality and subjectivity conventionally granted only to "round" characters, that is,
to characters capable of transcending such roles entirely. Bemused
by her own failure to be contained completely within her preordained niche, the significantly unnamed narrator of Rhys's short
story "Outside the Machine" mutters, "A born nurse, as they say.
Or you could be a born cook, or a born clown, or a born fool, a born

---

[15]The marked and delimited cases generally involve or invoke the school of fiction
called naturalism, which initially defined itself in terms of the protagonists' determination by the forces of heredity and environment. Interestingly, one of the key
texts of naturalist fiction, Emile Zola's *Nana*, is the book that Anna Morgan is reading
at the beginning of Rhys's *Voyage in the Dark* and perhaps serves as pre-text for the
action of that novel.
[16]Forster, *Aspects of the Novel*, p. 78.

this, a born that." When a neighbor asks her what the joke is, she replies, "Oh, nothing. I was thinking how hard it is to believe in free will."[17] The Rhys woman lives in a world where powerful and privileged people treat other people as if they were minor characters, born into and summed up by the supporting parts they play in the main drama. She is well aware that free will is an asset granted to those people who play leading roles, and aware in addition—the knowledge prompting responses ranging from irony to desperation—that the consciousness preventing her from somehow existing as a minor character in her own life places her outside the machine of both narrative and social conventions.[18]

For one of Rhys's most powerful insights is that categories of literary and social determination interpenetrate. If major characters tend to be "round" and thus not wholly predictable, they also tend to have privileges derived from some combination of gender, class, and racial factors that give them the scope to be masters of their fates. If minor characters tend to be "flat" and thus wholly predictable, they behave according to type inasmuch as they tend to *be* typed—by some combination of gender, class, and racial factors that denies them the scope to make changes in their own lives. The institution of feminist criticism has to a great extent been built on just this insight, for its project, like the projects of Marxist and Afro-American criticism, began with the enterprise of reading differently stories about characters who are not economically and socially privileged. Yet many feminist readers are also wary of stories that are, like Rhys's, "about victims," and they tend to express impatience especially with characters who internalize the terms of their oppression, as if such characters had only to resolve to adopt a better attitude in order to surmount whatever obstacles stood in their paths. This sort of reaction suggests that the belief in individual efficacy is such an important component of the novel's inherited value system that it can condition responses even of readers who

[17]Rhys, "Outside the Machine," in *Tigers Are Better Looking* (Harmondsworth, Eng.: Penguin, 1972), p. 90.

[18]I owe the phrase "minor character in her own life" to Alison Lurie's novel *Foreign Affairs* (New York: Random House, 1984), which plays on the same notion of a conventionally minor character (here an aging and unpretty woman who is actually named Vinnie Minor) in a major role.

are thoroughly trained in political analysis. Perhaps more provocatively, such a reaction also indicates that the novel is particularly successful in articulating and enforcing the limits of social tolerance. To borrow Rhys's phrase once again, novels communicate very well the terror consequent on being "outside the machine" because they intimate that the machine encompasses not only social and literary conventions but also the whole range of what is recognized as intelligible discourse.

Rhys's protagonists are victims who are fully aware of their victimization. Their awareness does not make them any less victimized; it serves only to make them self-conscious in their roles and thus alienated from the society that wants to identify them completely with these roles. Worst of all, because their situation as both marginalized and wholly conscious is impossible in the terms proposed by the dominant culture, the statements in which they express their awareness cannot have any acknowledged context. If they do not speak "in character," which is to say, in the wholly predictable ways that their role obliges, their utterances are received as senseless. To be outside the machine is to be without a language, condemned to emit sounds that inside interlocuters will interpret as evidence of duplicity, infantilism, hypocrisy—or simply madness.

To women writers—indeed, to women generally in Western tradition—the imputation of madness is a continual and potent threat, for madness is the possibility that haunts their cultural identity as Other. Because the masculinist point of view is by definition the rational and intelligible one, anybody occupying the cultural position of "woman" is at risk, required simultaneously to be a spokesman for this masculinist viewpoint and to embody its inverse or outside, the possibility of being *ir*rational, *un*intelligible. To express another point of view—to speak *as* "woman" in this culture—is to utter truths by convention so unimaginable that they are likely to be dismissed as gibberish, mere symptoms of hysteria.[19] Small wonder that female authors have been careful to mute or disguise their most subversive

[19]See Luce Irigaray, "The Blind Spot of an Old Dream of Symmetry," in *Speculum of the Other Woman*, trans. Gillian C. Gill (Ithaca: Cornell University Press, 1983), especially pp. 71–72.

insights and on occasion to attack women's writing that seems too flagrant in its violation of the accepted episteme.

The ultimate threat posed by imputations of madness is real madness, the prospect of a mind so riven by the pressure of condemnation and ridicule that it can no longer acknowledge what it knows. One of the central documents of current feminist criticism, Virginia Woolf's *Room of One's Own*, dramatizes the power of this threat in the narrative of Judith Shakespeare, William's hypothetical sister, who, with gifts equal to those of her brother, attempts to emulate his achievements. Woolf is initially detached in laying out the ways in which identical conditions aid William and thwart Judith, but at the climax of her exposition the cool, almost clinical tone gives way to an impassioned depiction of Judith's inevitable end:

> Any woman born with a great gift in the sixteenth century would certainly have gone crazed, shot herself, or ended her days in some lonely cottage outside the village, feared and mocked at. For it needs little skill in psychology to be sure that a highly gifted girl who had tried to use her gift for poetry would have been so thwarted and hindered by other people, so tortured and pulled asunder by her own contrary instincts, that she must have lost her health and sanity to a certainty.

Yet directly after this intensely moving passage, Woolf backs away from her own identification and outrage, asserting instead (and against the evidence of her own bravura prose) that such qualities can only damage writing: "Had she survived, whatever she had written would have been twisted and deformed, issuing from a strained and morbid imagination."[20] The lesson is clearly that open rebellion continues to exact too great a price. Not only will it be interpreted as madness, but eventually, ineluctably, it will produce madness.

This acute understanding of how insanity works as a cultural prohibition seems to underlie the frequently harsh judgments Woolf visits on her literary foremothers. In particular, her famous attack in *A Room of One's Own* on the novel that Gayatri Spivak has called

---

[20]Virginia Woolf, *A Room of One's Own* (New York: Harcourt Brace Jovanovich, 1957), pp. 51, 52.

"a cult text of feminism,"[21] Charlotte Brontë's *Jane Eyre*, seems informed by the awareness that one ought not to make one's meaning too evident. For in many respects the argument that Brontë advances through Jane's meditations is the same argument Woolf proposes through the example of Judith Shakespeare. The analogy is especially apparent when Woolf's persona, presenting herself as a reader of Brontë, quotes at length from the novel as a preliminary to commenting on it.

> "Women are supposed to be very calm but women feel just as men feel; they need exercise for their faculties and a field for their efforts as much as their brothers do; they suffer from too rigid a restraint, too absolute a stagnation, precisely as men would suffer; and it is narrow-minded in their more privileged fellow-creatures to say that they ought to confine themselves to making puddings and knitting stockings, to playing on the piano and embroidering bags. It is thoughtless to condemn them, or laugh at them, if they seek to do more or learn more than custom has pronounced necessary for their sex.
>
> "When thus alone I not infrequently heard Grace Poole's laugh . . . ."
>
> That is an awkward break, I thought. It is upsetting to come upon Grace Poole all of a sudden. The continuity is disturbed.[22]

Woolf suppresses here the revelation on which the plot of *Jane Eyre* will turn. The "continuity is disturbed" not by the servant Grace Poole but by the person whom Grace Poole was hired to guard, Mr. Rochester's mad wife, Bertha Mason. This "awkward break," which cuts off Jane's forthright demand that the (male) reader imaginatively empathize with women in their intolerable cultural role, is thus not Grace's but Bertha's laugh, the unintelligible utterance that serves to characterize a woman permanently outside the machine of accepted discourse. The threat of madness is so powerful in this passage that it prompts Woolf to read it back first into Charlotte Brontë's work and then, in an attribution more literary than historical, into Charlotte Brontë's life:

---

[21]Gayatri Chakravorty Spivak, "Three Women's Texts and a Critique of Imperialism," *Critical Inquiry* 12 (Autumn 1985), 244.

[22]Woolf, *Room*, p. 72.

The woman who wrote these pages had more genius in her than Jane Austen; but if one reads them over and marks that jerk in them, that indignation, one sees that she will never get her genius expressed whole and entire. Her books will be deformed and twisted. She will write in a rage where she should write calmly. She will write foolishly where she should write wisely. She is at war with her lot. How could she help but die young, cramped and thwarted?[23]

Brontë in fact died in the early stages of pregnancy, probably of untreated symptoms characterizing "morning sickness."[24] There are no grounds for interpreting her early death (or her small, "cramped" body) as a consequence of her "indignation." But the post hoc logic of Woolf's narrative[25] combines with an aesthetic desire for balance to make Brontë's end the equivalent of Judith Shakespeare's. The strain of resisting societal injunctions about what women can and cannot do leads to mangled work (if in fact the literary voice is not silenced entirely), to insanity, and to death: both women die of their writing. In the case of Brontë, however, the tragedy is complicated by the kind of writing she insists on doing. And the muffled theme of madness makes itself heard as a voice intruding into a meditation on blame.

Woolf's discussion of *Jane Eyre* begins, "I opened it at chapter twelve and my eye was caught by the phrase, 'Anyone may blame me who likes.' What were they blaming Charlotte Brontë for, I wondered?"[26] Technically, of course, this hypothesized blame, posited in order to be withdrawn, should attach to Jane, the narrator of the passage Woolf is quoting. Historically, as Woolf was well aware,

---

[23]Ibid., pp. 72–73.

[24]According to Philip Rhodes in "A Medical Appraisal of the Brontës" (*Brontë Society Transactions*, 16, no. 2 [1972], quoted in Helene Moglen, *Charlotte Brontë: The Self Conceived* [New York: Norton, 1976], p. 241 n. 20), "the evidence is quite clear that she died of hyperemesis gravidarum . . . an excess of the nausea and sickness which most women suffer in early pregnancy."

[25]And of narratives generally. As Roland Barthes notes, "Everything suggests, indeed, that the mainspring of narrative is precisely the confusion of consecution and consequence, what comes *after* being read in narrative as what is *caused by*; in which case narrative would be a systematic application of the logical fallacy denounced by Scholasticism in the formula *post hoc, ergo propter hoc*—a good motto for Destiny, of which narrative all things considered is no more than the 'language.' " "Structural Analysis of Narratives," in *Image/Music/Text*, trans. Stephen Heath (New York: Hill and Wang, 1977), p. 94.

[26]Woolf, *Room*, p. 71.

blame adhered to Charlotte Brontë, who in creating this protagonist gave voice to what contemporary critics called "an unregenerate and undisciplined spirit" and a "tone of mind and thought which has fostered Chartism and rebellion."[27] Woolf accordingly wants to maintain that the question of blame here is out of place, that a speaker should not be held personally culpable if she dares assert that the situation of women is insufferable. Nor, by the same token, should her speech be broken off by an insane woman's laughter, the parodic echo of her own unsanctioned anger. Yet the issue of rebellion has always been one of blame, for Woolf and for women generally, and inasmuch as rebellion is first construed as and then brings about madness, madness itself has traditionally been regarded as blameworthy. Indeed, the issue of blameworthy madness propels the plot of *Jane Eyre*, although the exposition of this theme is largely either tacit or muted by being subordinated to more manifest concerns. It was Jean Rhys, writing thirty years after the publication of *A Room of One's Own*, who made the theme central by allying madness with rebellion and making it the effect, not the cause, of her female protagonist's outcast status.

II

Wide Sargasso Sea, published in 1966, is Rhys's reinscription of *Jane Eyre*. Its protagonist is the same woman whose laugh—"distinct, formal, mirthless," in one of Jane's peculiarly precise descriptions[28]—disrupts Jane's meditations in order to enable the action of Brontë's novel, in the process motivating Virginia Woolf's complex ruminations on the subjects of madness, blame, and writing. By recentering the story on the character who is in many ways the most necessary accessory to the action—most necessary and most necessarily accessory—Rhys demonstrates how both social and narrative conventions mandate that certain categories of women

---

[27]Elizabeth Rigby, *Quarterly Review* (1848); and Anne Mozley, *Christian Remembrancer* (1853); both quoted in Sandra M. Gilbert and Susan Gubar, *The Madwoman in the Attic: The Woman Writer and the Nineteenth-Century Literary Tradition* (New Haven: Yale University Press, 1979), p. 337.

[28]Charlotte Brontë, *Jane Eyre* (London: Penguin, 1986), hereafter cited parenthetically in the text.

must be devalued if other categories of women are to assume importance.[29] This convention emerges as a source of considerable tension in the narrative.

"The lunatic is both cunning and malignant," Mr. Rochester tells Jane after he has been exposed as the husband of the women he is describing (*Jane Eyre*, p. 337), and the syntactical yoking of noun and adjectives is representative of the way in which disease and immorality tend to be conjoined in judgments about Bertha. Inasmuch as she is a lunatic, she is deprived of reason; indeed, she is so unreasoning as to be nonhuman. "It seemed, sir, a woman," Jane tells Rochester, describing Bertha's appearance in her room the night before the wedding is to take place, and her description concludes, "It reminded me . . . [of] the foul German spectre—the vampire" (p. 311). When she finally views the madwoman in broad daylight, she again seizes on the pronoun *it*: "What it was, whether beast or human being, one could not, at first sight tell: it grovelled, seemingly on all fours; it snatched and growled like some strange wild animal: but it was covered with clothing, and a quantity of dark, grizzled hair, wild as a mane, hid its head and face" (p. 321). And Rochester uses Bertha's nonhuman status to defend his choice of Jane: "Compare these clear eyes with the red balls yonder—this face with that mask—this form with that bulk" (p. 322).

Yet while the actions of this woman must be so alien to rational human concerns that they require no motives, she must also be responsible for these actions, or Rochester can have no moral authority for his attempted bigamy or his desire to be rid of her. Bertha must be not only a "lunatic" but also "cunning and malignant," a "demon" whose vampirish tendencies derive from her malevolence toward all humanity: "She said she'd drain my heart," her shaken brother reports after she has bitten him (p. 242). She must simultaneously be an evil person, one who is morally culpable for what

---

[29]Gayatri Spivak makes this point with political precision: "In this fictive England, [Bertha/Antoinette] must play out her role, act out the transformation of her 'self' into that fictive Other, set fire to the house and kill herself, so that Jane Eyre can become the feminist individualist heroine of British fiction. I must read this as an allegory of the general epistemic violence of imperialism, the construction of a self-immolating colonial subject for the glorification of the social mission of the colonizer. At least Rhys sees to it that the woman from the colonies is not sacrificed as an insane animal for her sister's consolidation" (p. 251).

she does, and subrational, subhuman. In particular, she must be without a human voice, because any reasons she might articulate could only suggest another side to the *Jane Eyre* story and undercut the premise that she is wholly dispensable.

In many respects, then, Bertha is the most marginal sort of character, for although she is absolutely necessary as a function, she must never be *heard*, in the sense of acknowledged to have made meaningful statements. She is outside the symbolic order by definition. Rhys commented perceptively that in *Jane Eyre* she is "a lay figure—repulsive, which does not matter, and not once alive, which does. She's necessary to the plot, but always she shrieks, howls, laughs horribly, attacks all and sundry—*off stage.*"[30] Not coincidentally, this offstage lay figure is also socially marginal because she is not a native Englishwoman. Like Rhys, she is a colonial from the West Indies. And in Brontë's novel the story of her origins colors Rochester's account of her madness and badness, to the point where madness, badness and creole origins are all equal figures for an essential pollution that must be exorcized from the fictional landscape.

Rhys believed that Charlotte Brontë had a special animus against West Indians, and certainly the two Jamaicans of *Jane Eyre* fare badly in comparison with the English.[31] In her initial impression of Bertha's brother, Richard Mason, Jane remarks "something in his face that displeased; or rather, that failed to please" and pinpoints this failing as a peculiarly foreign variety of spiritual flaccidity: "His features were relaxed, but too relaxed: his eye was large and well cut, but the life looking out of it was a tame, vacant life." Mason's habituation to a tropical climate and his consequent discomfort in the chill and damp of British winters (a trait shared by Rhys and all her Caribbean-born characters) becomes confirming evidence of his inherent weakness: "He occupied an arm-chair drawn close to the fire, and kept shrinking still nearer, as if he were cold" (p. 219). Rochester un-

---

[30]Letter to Selma Vaz Dias, 9 April 1958, *Letters*, p. 156.

[31]In a letter to Diana Athill in 1966, Rhys remarks in parentheses, "(I think too that Charlotte had a 'thing' about the West Indies being rather sinister places—because in another of her books 'Villette' she drowns the hero, Professor Somebody, on the voyage to Guadeloupe, another very alien place—according to her.)" (*Letters*, p. 297).

derscores all these implications later, after Mason has thwarted his marriage to Jane, when he cries, "Cheer up, Dick—never fear me!—I'd almost as soon strike a woman as you" (p. 320).

In the universe of *Jane Eyre*, then, a West Indian man is so effete as to be virtually a woman. A West Indian woman is an even more dubious phenomenon. Bertha's inherited contamination is at once female and racial: if "she came out of a mad family; idiots and maniacs through three generations," the source of this impurity was "her mother, the Creole" (p. 320). As foreigner and colonial, she is both unfamiliar and debased: Rochester reports finding "her nature wholly alien to mine, her tastes obnoxious to me, her cast of mind common, low, narrow and singularly incapable of being led to anything higher" (p. 333). And when in his narrative Bertha's manifold deficiencies are finally established as blameworthy as well as genetic, testimony not only to a diseased lineage but also to a self-motivated moral degeneration, the language that describes her debasement reflects prevailing European preconceptions about the landscape and inhabitants of the near-mythical islands that produced her: "Her character ripened and developed with frightful rapidity; her vices sprang up fast and rank.... What a pigmy intellect she had, and what giant propensities!" (pp. 333–34).

The West Indies themselves appear intrinsically fallen within the jingoistic economy of *Jane Eyre*. The "Wisdom" and "Hope" that Rochester regains after his disastrous marriage to Bertha come in the wake of "a wind fresh from Europe" that brings purgation: "The storm broke, streamed, thundered, blazed, and the air grew pure" (p. 335). Brontë was clearly concerned, however, that this nationalistic version of original sin would not suffice to establish Bertha as morally dispensable, even when augmented by her madness. Colonial origins may be tainted, but they are hardly things that Bertha has brought upon herself; similarly, Rochester affirms that madness per se is not ground for moral disgust when he tells Jane, "Your mind is my treasure, and if it were broken it would be my treasure still: if you raved, my arms should confine you and not a strait waistcoat" (p. 329). The combination of the two circumstances moves Bertha further into the margins, but it does not make her reprehensible until the admission of a third factor, about which Rochester can only hint. "Jane, I will not trouble you with abomi-

nable details; some strong words shall express what I have to say,"
he begins, and eschewing the details that were inappropriate for the
ears of Jane Eyre or the eyes of Brontë's readers, concludes, "Bertha
Mason, the true daughter of an infamous mother, dragged me
through all the hideous and degrading agonies which must attend
a man bound to a wife at once intemperate and unchaste" (pp. 333–
34).

"Unchaste" is of course the epithet that translates Bertha's victimization by uncontrollable external forces—racial and family heredity
and perhaps even physical disease (Joyce Carol Oates sees in Rochester's story evidence that Bertha "is suffering from the tertiary stage
of syphilis")[32]—into vice, still uncontrollable but now culpable.
Moral reprehensibility, which at first is merely insinuated as something implicit in the marginalizing factors of nationality and family
history, becomes Bertha's defining feature only when it is associated
with sensuality, which is treated as identical to promiscuity. Once
Rochester has established his wife as "unchaste," however, her las-
civiousness becomes conflated with her madness and is even represented as having preceded and brought on this madness: "Her
excesses had prematurely developed the germs of insanity" (p. 334).
In other words, the behavior for which Bertha is presumed to be
responsible, her sexual infidelity, is thoroughly confused with the
insanity that renders her repulsive to Rochester, with the consequence that she emerges as wholly responsible for her own repul-
siveness. The narrative desire that motivates the plot requires
this fuzzing of boundaries. What Oates calls Rochester's "curious
and ungentlemanly behavior regarding . . . the legitimate Mrs.
Rochester"[33] demands considerable vindication in a novel that is so
overtly *about* the injustice of blaming women for aspects of their lives
that are beyond their control. But by the same token, the charges
under which Bertha is condemned and banished cannot withstand
much in the way of direct scrutiny. For this reason, she remains
offstage, in the margins, the narrative analogue of her situation
within the story, locked away in the Thornfield attic.

[32]Joyce Carol Oates, "Romance and Anti-Romance: From Brontë's *Jane Eyre* to
Rhys's *Wide Sargasso Sea*," *Virginia Quarterly Review* 61, no. 1 (1985), 51.
[33]Ibid.

When in *Wide Sargasso Sea* the first Mrs. Rochester becomes the protagonist, the effect is to direct a spotlight at the shadowy borders of the *Jane Eyre* narrative. The Bertha of Rochester's story is exposed as a conceptual impossibility, with the consequence that she cannot be made to scuttle into corners to wait until her legal existence is no longer necessary to the plot. In particular, her taboo sensuality cannot be treated as something so grotesque and inappropriate as to cast her outside the pale of civilized interactions altogether. Under examination, the charge of "unchastity" tends to resonate uneasily with the eroticism of Jane's passion for Rochester, which fuels and directs the central action of Brontë's novel. Female sexual desire, the dirty secret that translates Bertha's victimization into blameworthiness, is also the source of Jane's power and the reason that her final triumph seems so richly deserved. Blanche Ingram, offered as the most explicit contrast, is found wanting precisely because she is incapable of wanting Rochester. The carefully maintained distinction between heroine and scapegoat blurs when the one is allowed to occupy the same narrative space as the other.[34]

In presenting the other side of the *Jane Eyre* story, Rhys exposes the culpability of Rochester's first wife as a function of narrative conventions: this woman behaves as she must in order to bring about a "euphoric" conclusion to a sequence of events wholly marginal to her own story. Moreover, as a central character she acquires motives, and these not only ground actions that already exist in the earlier book but exonerate her of blame in the process. For instance, a number of the causal relations implied in Rochester's account are reversed. Most significant, madness becomes a consequence of the wife's being cast out rather than a cause, and as a result the whole notion of insanity turns equivocal, meaning at once the way in which fury and frustration are construed by a masculinist audience and the way in which such fury and frustration prompt extremes of destructive (and necessarily self-destructive) behavior, as in the burning of Thornfield Hall. In the same way, the "unchastity" of Rhys's protagonist is the consequence rather than the cause of her husband's callousness and infidelity. In *Wide Sargasso Sea*, the wife

[34]Gilbert and Gubar discuss Bertha as Jane's "dark double" in *Madwoman*, pp. 356–62. See also Missy Dehn Kubitschek, "Charting the Empty Spaces of Jean Rhys's *Wide Sargasso Sea*," *Frontiers* 9, no. 2 (1987), 23–28.

turns to her cousin (the insult is compounded, in the man's eyes, by the fact that the cousin is mulatto) after her husband has copulated loudly with her own (black) maid in the adjoining room.

And in *Wide Sargasso Sea* it is the wife, not the husband, who is most evidently victimized by the institution of marriage. Brontë's Mr. Rochester proclaims of the woman he has just wrestled to the floor, "That is my *wife*. . . . Such is the sole conjugal embrace I am ever to know—such are the endearments which are to solace my leisure hours" (p. 322). But the madwoman of *Jane Eyre* was also an heiress; indeed, her wealth was the reason for the marriage in the first place. Rochester may be constrained from remarrying by the legal tie that binds, but this same tie allows him both the money and the authority to keep his wife prisoner in his attic. She has no resources or rights of her own, in fact no independent existence at all—a condition that Rhys points up when she has her most acute outsider, the black obeah woman Christophine, advise, "A man don't treat you good, pick up your skirt and walk out," only to discover that the "rich white girl" she counsels has been stripped of all her possessions under the terms of nineteenth-century English law.[35] Rochester's figurative entrapment corresponds to his wife's literal imprisonment, but the irony inherent in the contrast is suppressed in *Jane Eyre*, where the only woman endangered by Rochester's previous life must be Jane herself.

In these ways *Wide Sargasso Sea* provides, as Teresa O'Connor puts it, "an opposition to many of the givens of Brontë's novel."[36] But Rhys's revised version goes much further, not only countering the priorities that structure the value system of *Jane Eyre* but also revealing how narrative conventions that confine and finally eradicate Bertha are at the same time ways of bringing a rebellious female

---

[35]Rhys, *Wide Sargasso Sea*, in *Jean Rhys: The Complete Novels* (New York: Norton, 1985), p. 524, hereafter cited parenthetically in the text. Rhys was very clear about the historical conditions circumscribing Brontë's convenient madwoman and hypothesized that Brontë may well have known of such a woman in real life. "I believe and firmly too that there was more than one Antoinette," she wrote Francis Wydham in 1964. "The West Indies was (were?) rich in those days *for* those days and there was no 'married woman's property Act'. The girls (very tiresome no doubt) would soon once in kind England be *Address Unknown*. So gossip. So a legend." *Letters,* p. 271.
[36]O'Connor, *Jean Rhys,* p. 145.

protagonist back into the patriarchal fold. In order for *Jane Eyre* to reach its sanctioned "euphoric" conclusion, Jane's story must be incorporated into Rochester's story—and Jane must be incorporated into Rochester. Rochester's version of his own life and motives involves an attempt at bigamy that amounts to a betrayal of Jane, and thus his account must be regulated and corrected: he must admit and repent his transgressions. The process of emending his story is analogous to an act of contrition, in particular to cutting off the right hand that offends, and Rochester of course loses his right hand in the refining fire that prepares him to be united with Jane. But the union itself betrays Jane inasmuch as she has associated herself with the larger case of "women," and in particular it betrays her crucial meditation on the blame that society wrongly attaches to women for desiring freedom. Bertha's incarceration allows Jane to fall in love with Rochester; Bertha's escape terminates Jane's engagement; Bertha's death enables the marriage that constitutes the happy ending. But if Jane triumphs at the expense of Bertha, her triumph in turn shuts her up in the Rochester enclosure, for the "euphoric" ending is by definition one that terminates the story by locking away the female protagonist in the paternal house. "Reader, I married him," Jane reports, but for the reader her exultation may remain contaminated by the unease with which she had earlier contemplated the prospect of renouncing her name to assume the patronymic required to legitimate future children, the name of the father. "Soon to be Jane Rochester," Rochester had assured her, and she had felt "something stronger than was consistent with joy—something that smote and stunned; it was, I think, almost fear" (p. 287). Names both identify and constitute identity. The act of giving up the name under which one has known and been known is in many respects an act of consenting to become someone else. Charlotte Brontë clearly recognized this circumstance—for instance when she titled her novel not *Jane Rochester* but *Jane Eyre*.[37]

---

[37]Charlotte Brontë seems to have been alert to ways in which the prescribed "euphoric" conclusion of the heterosexual romance plot curtails identity and may not have been altogether easy about the ending of *Jane Eyre*. Certainly her next novel, *Villette*, goes to considerable lengths to avoid coming to a conclusion at all, leaving the options bifurcated between the "euphoric" termination involving marriage and a renunciation of the very palatable career as head of a school and a termination in

Jean Rhys also recognized the importance of names for women. In *Wide Sargasso Sea*, Bertha Antoinette Mason begins as Antoinette Cosway, daughter of Annette. (Ronnie Scharfman notes in the encoded matrilineage "a combination of Annette and 'toi': a hidden, built-in bond between mother and daughter.")[38] She acquires "Mason" through the superimposition of a stepfather and "Bertha" through her husband's Adam-like penchant for imposing his will by imposing his own colonizing language. "My name is not Bertha; why do you call me Bertha?" she asks the man, and he responds, "Because it is a name I'm particularly fond of. I think of you as Bertha," a palpable lie in the context of his first-person meditations, where he always refers to his bride as Antoinette (p. 540).

Furthermore, Rhys's novel suppresses the name of the father. The character in Rochester's position, prominent though he is in the plot and as a first-person narrator in the middle section of the book, remains carefully unnamed.)[39] His peculiar anonymity seems emblematic of the inverted hierarchies characterizing Rhys's revision of the *Jane Eyre* story, in which imperialist white male Europeans are irredeemably other, on the margins of a culture and even a nature that they are powerless to understand. If the West Indies were for Brontë a convenient fiction, they are too vivid, too present to Rhys's Rochester figure, who must insist finally on their unreality in order to sustain his own frantic assertion of European hegemony: "If these mountains challenge me, or Baptiste's face, or Antoinette's eyes, they are mistaken, melodramatic, unreal" (p. 519). At one point, however, he tells Antoinette, "This place is my enemy and on your

---

which the lover dies and the protagonist must perforce carry on with her teaching. The apostrophe in *Villette* that corresponds to "Reader, I married him" is "M. Emanuel was away three years. Reader, they were the three happiest years of my life." Charlotte Brontë, *Villette* (Harmondsworth, Eng.: Penguin, 1979), p. 593.

[38]Ronnie Scharfman, "Mirroring and Mothering in Simone Schwarz-Bart's *Pluie et Vent sur Telumée Miracle* and Jean Rhys's *Wide Sargasso Sea*," *Yale French Studies* 62 (1981), 103.

[39]Spivak notes, "His writing of the final version of the letter to his father is supervised, in fact, by an image of the *loss* of the patronymic," and goes on to quote from *Wide Sargasso Sea*, "There was a crude bookshelf made of three shingles strung together over the desk and I looked at the books, Byron's poems, novels by Sir Walter Scott, *Confessions of an Opium Eater*, some shabby brown volumes, and on the last shelf, *Life and Letters of* . . . The rest was eaten away" (*WSS*, p. 501, quoted in Spivak, "Three Women's Texts," 252). The missing name, Spivak notes, is likely to be Lord Rochester.

side" (p. 537), and the notion of an other side that menaces the secure vantage of the sanctioned white male point of view is what provokes so much of his rage against the islands and against his wife. For Antoinette it is England that is unreal, "a cold, dark dream" (p. 505), and even when she has arrived and has become the uneasy phantom of the attic, she maintains, "This cardboard house where I walk at night is not England" (p. 568). Indeed, for this woman England is necessarily a fiction—Brontë's fiction—and the "cardboard house" that contains her so completely is the already written account of her destiny, the novel between whose cardboard covers she is imprisoned.[40] In *Wide Sargasso Sea*, the Rochester character appropriates her for this house by appropriating her subjectivity, insisting first that she is his "marionette," who can serve as the repulsive "lay figure" of Rhys's description, and finally, at the conclusion of his first-person narrative, reducing her to the bare structural elements that the *Jane Eyre* plot requires: "I drank some more rum and, drinking, I drew a house surrounded by trees. A large house. I divided the third floor into rooms and in one room I drew a standing woman—a child's scribble, a dot for a head, a larger one for the body, a triangle for a skirt, slanting lines for arms and feet. But it was an English house" (p. 599). In *Wide Sargasso Sea* the English house, like English law, has only a paper existence. But paper in the hands of the oppressor is a formidable weapon in a world where paper entities have the power to confine people and to condition the universe that they inhabit. After her husband has concluded his account of her, Antoinette Cosway, rendered as a stick figure, enters an alien country to take her place as a prisoner of literary precedent.

III

If Antoinette Cosway in *Wide Sargasso Sea* has proved by far the most attractive and sympathetic of Rhys's protagonists, the attraction and sympathy are in many respects due to the historical documentation of the novel, to the fact that Antoinette is "emblematic of an entire way of life," as Oates observes: "If she is passive and easily victim-

---

[40]See also Spivak, "Three Women's Texts," pp. 50–51.

ized, this has been true of other members of the decayed Creole 'aristocracy' . . . ; if she suffers from a kind of sporadic amnesia, this too is typical of her people."[41] Her sufferings have clear external causes that correspond to a situation in the text known as history; most important, this situation is located far in the past, in the early nineteenth century, when a whole "people" can be explained without raising uncomfortable implications for present behavior. But she is also and concomitantly marginalized by another literary text, in ways suggesting that certain narrative conventions are inherently aligned with an ideology of marginality: of whom readers should and should not look at, of whose story is worth the telling, of what sorts of people ought to prove dispensable, means to an end. For this reason, her situation reflects on the situations of—and reader responses to—characters in earlier Rhys novels and implies that all Rhys's protagonists are to some degree prisoners of literary tradition.

The most thoroughly unsettling of the Rhys women is probably Julia Martin in *After Leaving Mr Mackenzie* (1930), who compounds the discomfort of dependency by being at a point in her life when she is aging out of successful objecthood. The title of the novel suggests the narrative impropriety of Julia's situation, an impropriety reinforced by the opening sentence: "After she had parted from Mr Mackenzie, Julia Martin went to live in a cheap hotel on the Quai des Grands Augustins."[42] The action in effect begins after the romance plot has concluded, concluded "dysphorically" inasmuch as the parting was initiated by Mr Mackenzie, who has withdrawn from his role as protector. Julia is hiding in the hotel, supported by a sort of pension doled out weekly by Mr Mackenzie's lawyer, "until the sore and cringing feeling, which was the legacy of Mr Mackenzie, had departed" (p. 238).

The burden of the plot is that Julia does not lose the sore and cringing feeling although she believes she ought to, indeed that she must. Her progress is steadily downward as she tries the remedies that have worked before, a change of man and then of location. She seems continually to sabotage her own efforts, for example lapsing

[41]Oates, "Romance and Anti-Romance," p. 54.
[42]Jean Rhys, *After Leaving Mr Mackenzie*, in *Jean Rhys: The Complete Novels*, p. 237, hereafter cited parenthetically in the text.

into indifference when she knows it is crucial to seduce Mr Horsfield, who has emerged as a possible protector, or exploding into resentment at the complacency of her Uncle Griffiths, whom she has attempted to approach for a loan. And the self-sabotage reflects an attitude presented early in the story, in an exchange with Mr Mackenzie after he has withdrawn his weekly stipend: "She said that she had fallen ill, and then she hadn't cared about anything except to lie in peace and be ill. And then she had written to the lawyer and asked for the allowance to be sent to her. And after that something had gone *kaput* in her, and she would never be any good any more—never, any more" (p. 251).

Mr Mackenzie's own point of view dominates the context of this explanation, and the passage is framed by his implicit diagnoses of hysteria, self-indulgence, and thoroughgoing bad taste. Earlier in the scene, the narrator formulated his general philosophy in such situations: "The secret of life was never to go too far or too deep. And so you let these people alone. They would be pretty certain to tell you lies, anyhow. And they had their own ways of getting along, don't you worry" (p. 248). Julia's apocalyptic claim that "she would never be any good any more—never, any more" emerges in this setting as clearly overdone, excessive, evidence of her lack of control, which is in turn evidence of her general unworthiness. Yet much later in the action, Julia accosts Mr Mackenzie again, and he confirms her claim that "something had gone *kaput* in her," although this time the judgment deals with her appearance: "She looked untidy. There were black specks in the corners of her eyes. Women go phut quite suddenly, he thought. A feeling of melancholy crept over him" (p. 343). Mackenzie thus articulates two basic positions about women and blame. On the one hand, he maintains that there can be no such thing as irremediable psychological damage to a woman who allows herself to be kept, and certainly not damage for which another person could in any way be held responsible. On the other hand, he maintains that aging inevitably produces in women sudden and irremediable *physical* damage, which removes them from any further consideration as objects of affection and thus of financial support. The two positions remain separate in his mind, and so he can treat Julia first with contempt and later with something like pity.

These judgments are, of course, equally dismissive; the action that informs the novel, although it never seems quite completed enough to warrant the "after," is *leaving* Mr Mackenzie. But just as Mr Mackenzie cannot nudge Julia entirely out of his field of vision, the reader is continually faced with a protagonist who seems as though she ought to be dismissed, either on the grounds that she has "gone phut" or on the grounds that she *believes* she has "gone phut" and therefore displays a bad attitude. No other Rhys woman has proved so discomfiting, or so susceptible to negative criticism—so much so that in the introduction to her edition of Rhys's complete novels, Diana Athill attempts to validate this criticism by assigning it to the author:

> Julia remembers catching butterflies when she was a child: how desperately she longed for their beauty, and how it was unfair of the grown-ups to scold her for damaging them when all she had intended was to keep them safe and happy in her jar. Julia remembers no more than her longing and her sense of injustice, but the reader is free to see that the butterflies died because the child's desire was blindly selfish. This passage of symbolism seems to me a flaw; but it does suggest that the reader who judges Julia severely is not doing so against the will of Jean Rhys.[43]

Julia is thereby convicted of "blindly selfish" desire that presumably continues from this inauspicious incident in her childhood and now informs her adult existence. Her conviction on this count implies authorial sanction for "the reader who judges Julia severely." But what does a severe judgment of Julia entail? What is Julia presumed to deserve?

What is at stake for Julia in *After Leaving Mr Mackenzie* is survival, her physical continuance as a living human being. That she survives is part of the extreme discomfort the novel produces in its readers, a discomfort accentuated by a passage that flirts with a "dysphoric" conclusion but evades it. Late in the action, Julia looks out at a patch of the Seine "where shadows danced and beckoned" until a gendarme accosts her, at which point she offers him the shopper's excuse, especially pertinent coming from a woman whose life as a commodity may be nearly over: "I was just looking" (pp. 338–39). She does not kill herself, although the whole context is such that

[43]Diana Athill, Introduction to *Jean Rhys: The Complete Novels*, pp. xi–xii.

her death would be a relief. In this narrative about female aging, continuity can only make matters worse, and Julia seems almost perverse in her desire to go on, "to intrude her sordid wish somehow to keep alive" into situations where she is profoundly unnecessary (p. 297). Yet she persists, despite the insistence of virtually all the other characters that she is not the *sort* of person who ought to survive any longer.

Athill's assertion that Rhys wants the reader to "judge Julia severely" appears an attempt to maintain that Julia is somehow to be regarded as having brought her situation on herself. Such a judgment would allow the reader to maintain a morally conditioned distance from the character, to withhold sympathy on the ground that the character has not earned it. But even granting the reader a detachment that Rhys's technique incessantly undermines, it seems difficult to hold to the notion that Julia should be so severely punished for her crime of selfishness, that she should be left to the humiliations of abject dependency foreshadowed in the figure of the old woman who lives upstairs in her hotel: "The woman had a humble, cringing manner. Of course, she had discovered that, having neither money nor virtue, she had better be humble if she knew what was good for her. But her eyes were malevolent—the horribly malevolent eyes of an old, forsaken woman. She was a shadow, kept alive by a flame of hatred for somebody who had long ago forgotten all about her" (p. 241). It may be significant that Athill makes this judgment when she is comparing Julia to her sister Norah. Equally trapped, equally resentful and terrified, Norah can lay claim to some altruism because she has devoted much of her adult life to taking care of their invalid mother. But the universe of *Mr Mackenzie* is not distinguished by altruism, and certainly the selfishness, or, more properly, the self-centeredness that Julia displays in the "symbolic" passage with the butterflies is a defining quality of all the male characters, even as all of them pass judgment on Julia.

Indeed, the charge of self-centeredness is most memorably leveled by Mr Mackenzie himself, during the confrontation scene Julia stages at the beginning of the story: "He listened, half-smiling. Surely even she must see that she was trying to make a tragedy out of a situation that was fundamentally comical. The discarded mistress—the faithful lawyer defending the honour of the client. . . . A situation consecrated as comical by ten thousand farces and a thousand comedies" (pp. 250–51). This reflection effectively conditions the tone of the subsequent encounter, tainting Julia's claim—"after that something had gone *kaput* in her, and she would never be any good any more—never, any more"—with the suspicion of self-dramatization and self-pity. But Mackenzie's bluff and worldly assessment of Julia's account—especially the imputation that her reading of her own situation involves a fundamental category mistake—relies on the "consecration" granted to their respective roles by literary precedent. The substance of Mr McKenzie's charge is not only that Julia has mistaken her genre but also that she has mistaken the nature and importance of her part: not only has she read her own story as a tragedy, whereas it is really a comedy or farce, but she has cast herself as the protagonist, whereas she really figures only as a peripheral, indeed, a stock character. These corrections to the context allow Mackenzie to reinscribe Julia's explanation in the register of banality, so that her protestations become the expected, if embarrassing, effusions of "these people." In a parallel scene later in the story, the younger and more sympathetic Mr Horsfield finds himself reflexively translating another of Julia's attempts to explain herself into the language of a comic music hall "turn":

> She began: "After all . . . " and then stopped. She had the look in her eyes of someone who is longing to explain herself, to say: "This is how I am. This is how I feel."
>   He suddenly remembered: "Pa was a colonel. I was seduced by a clergyman at a garden-party. Pa shot him. Heavens, how the blighter bled!" He wanted to laugh. [pp. 261–62]

In the course of the narrative, Mr Horsfield displays a certain amount of fellow feeling for Julia; later on he voices a central theme: "It's always so damned easy to despise hard-up people when in one way and another you're as safe as houses. . . . " (p. 284). But on this occasion the lines of banal dialogue seem to burst unbidden into his mind, asserting the existence of an already-written document within which Julia can be definitively placed and asserting his own identity as spokesman for the "safe as houses" cultural mainstream that has produced this document and ordained that it "consecrates" as comic or farcical certain predicaments involving certain categories of "hard-up people."

All of Rhys's novels, and many of her short stories, contain at least one character who performs this function of assuring the protagonist that literary tradition relegates her to the sidelines. Such assurances amount to a process of translation: the social forces that place people on the social margins are reconstrued as literary structures that reduce these same people to minor and indeed "flat" characters. In *Wide Sargasso Sea* the preexisting system of patriarchy is conflated with the already-written text of *Jane Eyre* to reduce Antoinette to a gendered stick figure within a symbolic enclosure. In *Mr Mackenzie*, the financial dependency of the aging, uneducated, professionless, inheritanceless, middle-class woman is interpreted as the matter of farce and secured with the title of "discarded mistress." In the novel published after *Mr Mackenzie*, *Voyage in the Dark* (1934), the nineteen-year-old Anna Morgan reports during the course of her first, devastating love affair, "Everybody says the man's bound to get tired and you read it in all books. But I never read now, so they can't get at me like that, anyway."[44] But the network of respectable businessmen that has already incorporated Anna into the sexual underclass serving as its harem insists that she must accept its reading of her situation. As her lover's cousin writes in the letter ending the affair, the issue has not been one of love at all, *"especially that sort of love—and the more people, especially girls, put it right out of their heads and do without it the better"* (p. 58). If Anna has been used, her option is to "get on" in the prostitution business, counsel that bewilders her because she has never felt she chose that particular profession and sees no reason to *want* to "get on" in it. But the sanction for the official version of her predicament comes, once again, from literature. The letter continues, *"Do you remember when we talked about books? I was sorry when you told me that you never read because, believe me, a good book like that book I was talking about can make a lot of difference to your point of view. It makes you see what is real and what is just imaginary"* (p. 58). At the opening of the novel, Anna's

---

[44]*Voyage in the Dark*, in *Jean Rhys: The Complete Novels*, p. 46, hereafter cited parenthetically in the text.

fellow chorus girl, Maudie, remarked of the book that Anna was reading (Zola's *Nana*, the title an anagram of Anna's own name), "I know; it's about a tart. I think it's disgusting. I bet you a man writing a book about a tart tells a lot of lies one way and another. Besides, all books are like that—just somebody stuffing you up" (pp. 4–5). This view of literary tradition as a means by which privileged men systematically lie to and about the women they exploit permeates *Voyage in the Dark*, to the point where the relation of "unrespectable" women to written language becomes intensely problematic. After her rejection, Anna sits in bed compulsively writing and tearing up letters to her former lover, finally lapsing into a sort of stream-of-consciousness style ("writing very quickly, like you do when you write") to insist on the reality of her own emotions: "My dear Walter I've read books about this and I know quite well what you're thinking but you're quite wrong because don't you remember you used to joke because every time you put your hand on my heart it used to jump well you can't pretend that can you you can pretend everything else but not that it's the only thing you can't pretend" (p. 64). But obviously her mustering of the physical evidence supporting her claim to be in love with Walter cannot convince, indeed will be read as largely irrelevant, within a sexual economy where her acceptance of financial support makes her (to borrow once again the mutually exclusive categories in which Elgin Mellown has couched a dichotomy "consecrated" by literary precedent) "essentially a mercenary."

The "translators" who reinscribe the protagonists' situations into terms hallowed by the writing of the dominant culture are so pervasive and so powerful in Rhys's novels that they guarantee the protagonists cannot make their stories *heard* within their own fictional universes. To be heard—to be acknowledged as having uttered meaningful statements—these protagonists would have to be recognized as possessing subjectivity, even an independent existence, within a regulative structure that grants them neither. For this reason, their own testimony to the contrary must continually be referred back to the already written. Thus Julia and Anna, conventionally "women with a past," are not allowed to have their own histories. Their personal backgrounds are inadmissible *because* personal, uniquely their own. The people most concerned to use them as supporting characters need to render them generic, to turn them not only into "flat" characters but into potentially interchangeable versions of a single type.

The process begins immediately in *Voyage in the Dark* when Anna and Maudie are approached on the street by a Mr Jones and a Mr Jeffries. Mr Jeffries, later the "Walter" of Anna's torn-up letters, asks Anna's age and discovers that she is eighteen. At this point, Mr Jones provides a gloss palpably intended to counter any suggestion that Anna is innocent or ingenuous and thus to counter the effect this woman is producing on his friend. "He knew you'd be either eighteen or twenty-two. You girls only have two ages. You're eighteen and so of course your friend's twenty-two. Of course" (pp. 6–7). The phrases "you girls" and "of course" reduce Anna's real age to a lie, attributed to the calculated production of a self-stereotype. More disturbing, they tend to suggest that *any* age claimed by either of these women will likewise be a lie, that the number of years between such a woman's birth and the present moment can exist *only* as an attribute that she puts on, like makeup or clothing, to make herself desirable to a prospective buyer. Inasmuch as these women are viewed primarily as commodities, their defining features are presumed to be responses to the market: supply created solely in order to satisfy demand.

The process of "translation" is most devastating in contributing to the alienation of Anna from her West Indian past. Traumatically orphaned, removed from her homeland and taken to England by her repressively respectable stepmother—the opening sentence of the novel, "It was as if a curtain had fallen, hiding everything I had ever known" (p. 3), places narrative emphasis on the catastrophic break in her sense of personal continuity—Anna finally becomes so detached from identification with her childhood, family, or indeed any sort of belonging that her past can only enter into her present consciousness through the violent disruptions of involuntary memory. (Rhys highlights the estrangement by putting associatively remembered incidents, like the passages of writing from letters, in italics.) Her interactions with the men who use her for sexual entertainment serve to intensify the split. For example, despite some evidence of personal concern (based largely on her virginity when he met her, "the only thing that matters," as he assures her before the defloration [p. 22]), Walter is completely uninterested in her

Caribbean background and tends either to mechanically "reflect" back her statements about her heritage or to treat them with gentle ridicule. Her subsequent lovers go from dismissing to overtly revising her account of origins, as when an American named Joe claims to "know" about her country and her family:

> He sat on the bed. "I know, I know. Trinidad, Cuba, Jamaica—why, I've spent years there." He winked at Laurie.
>
> "No," I said, "a little one."
>
> "But I know the little ones too," Joe said. "The little ones, the big ones, the whole lot."
>
> "Oh, do you?" I said, sitting up.
>
> "Yes, of course I do," Joe said. He winked at Laurie again. "Why, I knew your father—a great pal of mine. Old Taffy Morgan. He was a fine old boy, and didn't he lift the elbow too."
>
> "You're a liar," I said. "You didn't know my father. Because my real name isn't Morgan and I'll never tell you my real name and I was born in Manchester and I'll never tell you anything real about myself. Everything that I tell about myself is a lie, so now then."
>
> He said, "Well, wasn't his name Taffy? Was it Patrick, perhaps?" [p. 78]

Joe's winks, directed at Anna's more cynical friend Laurie, serve the same function as Mr Jones's earlier phrases "you girls" and "of course." They acknowledge what is presumed to be a mutual awareness of Anna's evident self-fabrication. Here the question is even less one of hiding the truth about Anna, of veiling her real story in more glamorous trappings: Joe's dubiety about Anna's "little" island does not imply a parallel certainty about her origins in a prosaic place like Manchester. In fact, Joe seems to appropriate Anna's account of her antecedents and make it deliberately generic ("Taffy" is a stock nickname for Welshmen just as "Patrick" is a stock name for Irishmen, a similarly debased minority in England) on the assumption that his version is just as good as hers, if not better because he has the power in this relationship. The assumption forces Anna into a posture of total denial. She responds with a variation on the Cretan paradox ("Everything that I tell you about myself is a lie, so there now"), which is intended to protect her endangered sense of identity from further damage but which in effect confirms her own words to be as meaningless as Joe takes them to be.

In a very similar manner, Julia in *After Leaving Mr Mackenzie* appears to have lost control over her own past, and thus to have lost her sense of individual identity, through lack of an audience willing to hear and believe her own story. Very early in the delineation of a highly circumscribed fictional universe, whose reputable inhabitants are clearly tagged and shelved (for instance, her sister Norah is "labelled for all to see . . . 'Middle class, no money' " [p. 275]), the narrator introduces Julia as someone who is significantly unlabeled: "Her career of ups and downs had rubbed most of the hall-marks off her, so that it was not easy to guess at her age, her nationality, or the social background to which she properly belonged" (p. 240). The implication that Julia has somehow *become* generic as the consequence of a "career of ups and downs" acquires substance in an important passage that has storytelling as its subject. Julia describes to Mr Horsfield a period in her life when she worked as a mannequin for a female sculptor, and this story in turn becomes the frame for the story of how she lost faith in her own stories:

> And so one day, when we were sitting smoking, and having tea, I started to tell her about myself. I was just going to tell her why I left England. . . . One or two things had happened, and I wanted to go away. Because I was fed up, fed up, fed up.
>
> I wanted to go away with just the same feeling a boy has when he wants to run away to sea—at least, that I imagine a boy has. Only, in my adventure, men were mixed up, because of course they had to be. You understand, don't you? Do you understand that a girl might have that feeling? . . .
>
> And when I had finished I looked at her. She said: "You seem to have had a hectic time." But I knew when she spoke that she didn't believe a word. [pp. 263–64]

It is particularly important that a female interlocuter refuses to acknowledge the reality of Julia's story, for within Rhys's fictional parameters only women have the capacity to understand that there might *be* such a thing as female desire or experience. Throughout *Mr Mackenzie*, Julia seeks out women who appear sympathetic, manifestly searching for the kind of acceptance she associates with the mother who long ago was "the warm centre of the world" for her (p. 294). But women prove to be spokesmen for the masculinist viewpoint in this novel, and as spokesmen they uphold a societal edict to the effect that male and female experiences cannot be compared, not merely because the realms of masculine and feminine endeavor are far apart but because female experience as such is unimaginable. When Julia aligns her adolescent desire to get away from England with a boy's desire to run away to sea, her analogy acts as a socially conditioned cue that triggers an attitude of blank incomprehension. Later in the narrative, she tries to tell a former lover about her "career of ups and downs" and is met with a show of jolly acceptance. "I've got a lot of mad friends now," Mr James assures her. "I call them my mad friends." But when Julia presses him, "People who haven't got on? . . . Men?" he recoils from any understanding of Julia's situation that further empathy might entail: "Oh, no, some women too. Though mind you, women are a different thing altogether. Because it's all nonsense; the life of a man and the life of a woman can't be compared. They're up against entirely different things the whole time. What's the use of talking nonsense about it? Look at cocks and hens; it's the same sort of thing,' said Mr James" (p. 299). The point is driven home firmly a few pages further, when Julia escapes for a time into a movie theater. "After the comedy she saw young men running races and some of them collapsing exhausted. And then—strange anti-climax—young women ran races and also collapsed exhausted, at which the audience rocked with laughter" (p. 301). In Rhys's world, gender cues genre. The activity that signals heroic aspiration in men is the stuff of farce when women attempt it. The spectacle of defeat is coded as ludicrous when it involves characters so marginal to the great central movements of the drama that nothing they do could be read as triumph.

Because other inhabitants of her universe refuse to hear her, Julia loses her own sense of having *come from* anywhere, of having a continuous identity that extends back into the past and can extend forward toward anything resembling a goal. Without validation from the outside world, even tangible evidence cannot assure her that the story of her life is not simply another fabricated, detachable aspect of her existence as a commodity:

> Then we went out to dinner. When I got home I pulled out all the photographs I had, and letters and things. And my marriage-book and my passport. And the papers about my baby who died and was buried in Hamburg.

But it had all gone, as if it had never been. And I was there, like a ghost. [p. 265]

Mutilated by the process of being reduced to a "flat" character, Julia is alternately affectless and desperate, resigned to a preordained destiny and furious at the "respectable" people who take credit for their own effortless lives. In living by her appearance she has been condemned to the impossible existence of *being* appearance. Like the woman in a Modigliani print hanging in the sculptor's studio, her role is to be nothing but body, and as she stares at the picture she feels as if it were saying, "I am more real than you. But at the same time I *am* you. I am all that matters of you" (p. 224).

All the Rhys women get this message in one form or another, despite significant differences in the way protagonists and supporting characters are presented. In the course of writing her five novels, Rhys developed three distinct narrative strategies. In *Quartet* (1928) and *Mr Mackenzie,* she uses a third-person narrator and a multiple point of view that can shift, often disconcertingly, from the mind of the protagonist to the minds of the people with whom she is immediately involved. In *Voyage in the Dark* and *Good Morning, Midnight* (1939), she uses a first-person narrative voice limited to the protagonist herself, with other voices emerging only through the protagonist's conversations and recollections. In *Wide Sargasso Sea,* she uses two first-person narrators, with Antoinette speaking in the first and third chapters and her husband delivering the central chapter. Yet despite the disparities in method, all the novels manage the difficult feat of presenting characters who are obviously powerful enough to ensure the protagonist's marginality in her own world, while remaining minor from the point of view of the reader.

It is important to note the difficulty of this achievement precisely because a number of critics have faulted Rhys for her "unsympathetic" supporting characters, especially the male ones. Except for the Rochester figure, none of the men is explained, justified, or given anything much in the way of motivation; each simply exploits or judges the protagonist with the confidence of someone engaging in a habitual or customary activity. Of course, Rhys's novels are eminently about exploitation and judgment and in particular about how the two are often identical. And as the preceding discussion may begin to indicate, exploitation and judgment are encoded in the already-written texts of the dominant culture, so that when representatives of that culture banish one of Rhys's protagonists to its margins, they are merely restoring an order so pervasive that they cannot question its prescriptions. In this context, habit and custom emerge as the most credible—and the most terrifying—motives.

Moreover, the privileged male characters appropriate and express positions that readers might otherwise feel free to take. In using their social and political power to assign a name to the protagonist and control the meaning of her speech and actions, such characters make visible the mechanisms that render her marginal. As a consequence, it becomes impossible for readers to assume that judgments blaming this protagonist for her own situation and/or dismissing her entirely from serious consideration are politically neutral, separable from the power structure that governs her. One judges the Rhys woman "severely," in Diana Athill's words, at the risk of colluding with the system that enforces her marginality.

The disorienting, uncomfortable quality of Rhys's writing derives finally from Rhys's exposure of the easy and ready-to-hand interpretation as an ideological construct. This interpretation is always represented in her novels, either through the coercive speech of one or more of the privileged characters or—in the case of *Wide Sargasso Sea*—through allusions to a particular canonized literary text, which by already existing makes the protagonist's victimization and sacrifice inevitable. By making it an untenable interpretation, Rhys closes off the possibilities for dismissing the marginal woman who exists so disconcertingly at the center of her narratives, and opens up the possibility that someone may yet hear the other side of an old, familiar story.

Chapter 2

The Future in a Different Shape: Broken Form and Possibility in *The Golden Notebook*

The Golden Notebook, first published in 1962, is a novel preoccupied with its own situation as contemporary fiction. Most obviously, it is concerned with its relation to bourgeois realism and modernism, and it incorporates discussions of both traditions into the various levels of its fictional discourse while undermining realist and modernist assumptions about the necessary hegemony of such levels. Perhaps less evidently, it is concerned with its relation to the older tradition of encyclopedic narrative, in which the entire range of knowledge and beliefs peculiar to a culture is comprehended and systematized, and it represents a deliberate attempt to encompass "most of the ideas we take for granted," which were in fact "born with the French Revolution," as Lessing subsequently explained in an interview.[1] And it is vitally concerned with its relation to the ambiguous tradition of "women's writing" and sensitive to the political nature of the double bind constraining a female novelist who attempts either to continue in or to dissociate herself from this tradition. In short, it is a highly self-conscious and experimental work, and the fact that both its self-consciousness and its experimentation were ignored for most of the decade after its publication argues both

[1] Florence Howe, "A Conversation with Doris Lessing (1966)," in *Doris Lessing: Critical Studies*, ed. Annis Pratt and L. S. Dembo (Madison: University of Wisconsin Press, 1974), p. 7. For a discussion of encyclopedic narrative, see Ronald T. Swigger, "Fictional Encyclopedism and the Cognitive Value of Literature," *Comparative Literature Studies* 12 (December 1975), 351–66.

for the volatility of its subject matter and for the tenacity of critical presuppositions. During the 1960s and much of the 1970s reviews and critical articles dealing with *The Golden Notebook* regularly conflated separate characters, elided carefully distinguished plots, and glossed over flagrant contradictions, so that Lessing's most ambitious fiction was in effect reduced to formal conventionality.[2] *The Golden Notebook* was widely praised and influenced the thinking of a whole generation of female readers, but at the same time there was little critical understanding of what *kind* of novel it is.

Yet *The Golden Notebook* repeatedly addresses the question of its own generic self-definition. A passage of dialogue near the beginning of the first "Free Women" segment, for example, suggests some of the immediate consequences of assigning a work too quickly to received categories. Noting the attitudes that have apparently prevented Anna from producing a second novel, Molly observes plaintively, "After all, you aren't someone who writes little novels about the emotions. You write about what's real." Anna reacts to the banality of the catchphrase "little novels about the emotions," but despite her conviction that "many of the things we say are just echoes" and her judgment that her friend's remark "is an echo from communist party criticism—at its worst moment, moreover," she feels obliged to respond: "If marxism means anything, it means that a little novel about the emotions should reflect 'what's real' since the emotions are a function and a product of society. . . . "[3] The ellipses signal her uncertainty, for the need to assert a seamless continuity between "the emotions" and "what's real" tacitly acknowledges that the distinction is a meaningful one; in point of fact,

---

[2]Most reviewers seem to have begun from assumptions about the form and then come up with a reading that fits the assumptions. Robert Taubman is representative. Taubman expresses the hope that *The Golden Notebook* "will soon displace the Simone de Beauvoir paperbacks in the hands of all those who want what she is supposed to provide—a sort of intelligent woman's guide to the intelligent woman"; he notes an "unusual structure" but believes it to be "less a matter of subtle organization than of simple, rather haphazard naturalism." He closes the subject with the observation, "If there is anything new here, then it is an advance in naturalism; but in the sort of naturalism . . . that tends to devalue its object" (*New Statesman*, 20 April 1962, reprinted in *On Contemporary Literature*, ed. Richard Kostelanetz [Plainview, N.Y.: Books for Libraries Press, 1964], pp. 402–3).

[3]Doris Lessing, *The Golden Notebook* (New York: Bantam, 1981), p. 42, hereafter cited parenthetically in the text.

it was extremely important for the reception of fiction during the postwar period *The Golden Notebook* chronicles. By the standards of those contemporaries who exerted most influence over Anna—and over Lessing, at least while she subscribed to the party line on literature—to write about the personal, the individual, the realm of "the emotions" was to descend into triviality; it was to fall short of the ideals of objectivity and comprehensiveness implied in the equation of "what's real" with conventional realism.

The equation was explicitly ideological. The debate over ways to resuscitate the realist novel was the focal point of Marxist literary aesthetics in Western Europe during the mid-1950s, and the persistence of the kind of writing that Molly dismisses as "little novels about the emotions" impressed British communists as evidence of regression to an antihumanism the more regrettable because it represented a division within the realist project itself. For Jack Lindsay, one of the most articulate of the orthodox critics of the period and a longtime friend of Lessing's,[4] true art was essentially bound up with the external world and with social change; was both "a form of knowing and mastering reality" and "that which advances life." In terms of this fundamentally mimetic theory any kind of formal experimentation is by definition aberrant; modernism is thus merely "one aspect of the disintegration of our culture under imperialism," representing "the way in which components of an art-form break up as things-in-themselves and fail to blend in the proportions that produce great art." But because in such a theory disintegration and particularity are the chief enemies, a realism that restricts itself to rendering a part or aspect of the historical continuum, which is postulated as the ultimate context of human experience, is similarly antithetical to human progress. In Lindsay's view the contemporary writer must achieve "a new kind of unifying vision, a new sense of dynamic interconnections and of the position of the individual in history" in order to achieve an art form that is the aesthetic equivalent of the social force by whose agency "human unity can be realised . . . *the organised proletariat.*"[5]

---

[4]She contributed an affectionate poem, "Dear Jack," to the volume privately printed on the occasion of his eightieth birthday, *A Garland for Jack Lindsay*, ed. James Corbett (London: Piccolo Press, 1980), n.p.

[5]Jack Lindsay, *After the Thirties: The Novel in Britain and Its Future* (London: Lawrence

Raymond Williams, probably the foremost Marxist cultural theorist in England at the time, was even more insistent on the retro-
grade character of "little novels about the emotions," which he
regarded as reversions to an "immature" realism. His emphasis in
his classic study *The Long Revolution* is also on unity, specifically on
synthesizing personal and social aspects of experience and thus rein-
tegrating "personal" and "social" novels into a more inclusive
whole; and the terms in which he couches his discussion are strikingly similar to those Anna chooses when she describes "the only
kind of novel which interests me: a book powered with an intellectual
or moral passion strong enough to create order, to create a new way
of looking at life" (p. 61), and when she yearns for a Marxism that
will bring "an end to the split, divided, unsatisfactory way we all
live" (p. 161). "When I think of the realist tradition in fiction,"
Williams writes, "I think of the kind of novel which creates and
judges the quality of a whole way of life in terms of the qualities of
persons. . . . Every aspect of personal life is radically affected by the

---

and Wishart, 1956), pp. 146–47, 187, 223–24, 161. Lindsay's position derives from the
very influential work of Georg Lukács; for a synopsis of Lukács's valorization of
realism as both rigorously selective and absolutely comprehensive see "Narrate or
Describe?" in *Writer and Critic and Other Essays* (New York: Grosset and Dunlap, 1970),
pp. 110–48. The utopian note of the last passage quoted from Lindsay's study is
especially poignant in view of the fact that this book came out just before Soviet tanks
entered Budapest, definitively ending Western optimism about the progressive nature
of communism in the Soviet Union. Lessing's one overtly propagandistic novel,
Retreat to Innocence (London: Michael Joseph, 1956), published in the same year,
contains an inadvertently pathetic minor character who is deciding whether to leave
England and return to her native Hungary, a choice that subsequent events immediately made irrelevant. *Retreat to Innocence* considers the contrast between old leftists
who grew up participating in the great antifascist movements of the 1930s and 1940s
and the new, apathetic generation coming of age in the 1950s, and in this respect
foreshadows the Molly-Tommy conflicts in *The Golden Notebook*. But this similarity is
probably less important than the striking differences between the two novels. *Retreat
to Innocence* espouses a view of history as an uninterrupted series of advances since
the 1917 revolution and celebrates through one of its two central characters, a middle-
aged Eastern European writer, the kind of novel that Lessing upheld in her 1957
essay "The Small Personal Voice" and implicitly repudiated in *The Golden Notebook*;
as the (apolitical, wrong) other central character reports, it is "one of those awful
novels with a thousand characters all talking at once . . . an incident in every para-
graph, and the action taking place in a dozen countries simultaneously. It's all so
old-fashioned!" (*Retreat to Innocence*, p. 231). Many of the passages in *The Golden
Notebook* dealing with the party line on literature, especially the parodies of those
books summed up as "an honest novel of Party life" (p. 347), seem to be reactions
against *Retreat to Innocence*.

quality of general life, yet the general life is seen at its most important in completely personal terms."[6] Lorna Sage observes that this kind of statement is almost "a synopsis for *The Golden Notebook*," which places personal relations in a context so global that even the early volumes of the *Children of Violence* series, with their avowed commitment to "a study of the individual conscience in its relations with the collective," seem parochial by comparison.[7] Hardly a "little novel" by anyone's criteria, it continually urges the necessity of making connections and seeing things whole, processes that might seem to involve putting the emotions firmly in their place within an encompassing interpretive structure—in terms of Anna's renovated Marxism, making them "a function and a product of society." In certain respects it thus appears to stand as an exemplary response to the manifestos of Lindsay and Williams, forging a new order, insisting on the necessity of integration, and reasserting the claims of humanist aesthetics. Yet it is not itself ordered or integrated in terms of the realism that Lindsay and Williams are concerned to uphold, and in its systematic repudiation of traditional Marxism it expressly repudiates the whole critical and ideological stance implied in Molly's formulation "what's real." If it places "the personal" within a social and historical context, it is not by that token identified with theories maintaining that only subordination to this sort of context can grant "the personal" any significance. And this last point is important, because the phrase "little novels about the emotions" has connotations that Marxist theory of the period does not acknowledge and perhaps does not even recognize. In their ostensible triviality and concern with the private sphere, such "little novels" are likely to be both by and about women, to be, in other words, that dubious phenomenon "women's writing."

Some of what is at stake in this distinction between "the emotions" and "what's real" becomes apparent in Irving Howe's 1962 review,

[6]Raymond Williams, *The Long Revolution* (London: Chatto and Windus, 1961), p. 278.

[7]Lorna Sage, *Doris Lessing* (London: Methuen, 1983), p. 45; Doris Lessing, "The Small Personal Voice," in *A Small Personal Voice: Essays, Reviews, Interviews* (New York: Vintage, 1974), p. 14. Sage's book contains an excellent discussion of the ideological presuppositions of realism, as does Jenny Taylor's introductory essay, "Situating Reading," in *Notebooks/Memoirs/Archives: Reading and Rereading Doris Lessing*, ed. Jenny Taylor (Boston: Routledge and Kegan Paul, 1982), pp. 1–42.

which was influential in generating a widespread readership for *The Golden Notebook* in the United States. Howe virtually recapitulates the distinction, although in his absorption with the "fierce attachment to 'personal values' " that he, like Lindsay and Williams, sees as characteristic of novels "in recent years," he does not seem to notice the extent to which Lessing's characters have anticipated him. He accordingly commends the novel in familiar terms: Lessing understands that "the idea of 'personal relations' has been shaped by the catastrophes of our time and, in the form we know it, is not to be taken as an absolute or uncontaminated value." Not content with intimations, however, he goes on to reveal what kind of writer *is* guilty of exalting "personal relations" to undeserved eminence, in a passage worth quoting at some length:

> Miss Lessing has a voice and a mind of her own. She is radically different from other women writers who have dealt with the problems of their sex, first in that she grasps the connection between Anna Wulf's neuroses and the public disorders of the day, and second in that she has no use either for the quaverings of the feminist writers or the aggressions of those female novelists whose every sentence leads a charge in the war of the sexes. The feminine element in *The Golden Notebook* does not become a self-contained universe of being, as in some of Virginia Woolf's novels, nor is the narrative voice established through minute gradations of the writer's sensibility, as in some of Elizabeth Bowen's. And Miss Lessing is far too serious for those displays of virtuoso bitchiness which are the blood and joy of certain American lady writers.[8]

The hostility of this diatribe seems to derive from the assumption that "women's writing"—not only writing by women but also writing that takes female experience as its primary subject matter—is a distinct and self-evidently inferior genre that perversely refuses to acknowledge its own mediocrity. If possession of "a voice and a mind of her own" allows Lessing to transcend the norm of "women writers who have dealt with the problems of their sex," in the process she has transcended a collection of stereotypically feminine attributes: inability to see the big picture or make abstract connections (such as "the connection between Anna Wulf's neuroses and the

---

[8]Irving Howe, "Neither Compromise nor Happiness," *New Republic*, 14 December 1962, 17.

public disorders of the day"), obsession with minutiae of the "sex war" (manifested as either "quaverings" or "aggressions"), immersion in the immediate and by implication domestic present (Woolf's "self-contained universe of being"), hypersensitivity (Bowen's "minute gradations of . . . sensibility"), or bitchiness (the "American lady writer" that Howe has in mind is surely Mary McCarthy). Her achievement has been to treat the sphere of "personal relations" that has traditionally been the province of "women's writing" in a way that presumes a governing structure of serious, "real" concerns. In order to bestow this accolade Howe is driven to misread Lessing's novel drastically, conflating the two "breakdown" stories along with the male characters involved in them and taking the end of "Free Women" for the conclusion of the entire narrative.[9] The misreading is virtually required by the terms of his admiration. Lessing writes about "what's real" and therefore must write the kind of realist novel to which he harks back with thinly veiled nostalgia.[10] In doing so she surpasses expectation, rising above the conditions that hamper female authors generally and in particular those female authors who persist in dealing with the topic of female experience.

Howe thus applauds *The Golden Notebook* in terms that *The Golden Notebook* itself calls into doubt and sets Lessing above other women writers with the same imperviousness to irony that he manifests in accepting without question that Anna and Molly belong above the normal run of unfree women. By contrast, the development of the "Free Women" narrative within the novel forces the recognition that the benefits of tokenism accrue chiefly to the men who read "free" as "available," so that the relative independence of the protagonists emerges as merely another sort of constraint. Lessing is fully aware

[9]Ibid., pp. 18–20. There are other substantive errors. Howe claims that Anna is "reduced to hysteria by a disastrous affair with an egomaniacal American writer," thus taking occasion for cause and completely missing the central trope of "madness" as insight; and he decries the "loss of critical objectivity [Lessing] had maintained in earlier pages" in the Blue and Golden notebook descriptions of "breakdown," completely overlooking the critique of such "objectivity," which suggests it may not be a self-evident desideratum.

[10]That this is also Anna's nostalgia in the Blue notebook, and that it was Lessing's own nostalgia when she embraced the orthodox Marxist view of literature—during the time of "The Small Personal Voice," for instance—is very much to the point of what Lessing is doing with literary history in *The Golden Notebook*.

of how equivocal is any privilege that raises her above all the rest of her sex, especially when the basis for this privilege is a purely negative one, such as having *avoided* writing a "little novel about the emotions." If some of the remarks in the preface she wrote for the reissue of *The Golden Notebook* ten years after its initial publication suggest that she is uncomfortable with readings taking "the sex war" as her primary or sole focus, her insistence that "the essence of the book, the organisation of it, everything in it, says implicitly and explicitly that we must not divide things off, must not compartmentalise" does not specify a kind of holism in which women's issues are exposed as partial and minor by being subordinated to an overarching intellectual framework.[11] Indeed, the unity that results when the individual and the personal are subsumed under a governing premise is precisely what *The Golden Notebook* seems most interested in questioning. Such a unity is necessarily static, with no potential for development, because it postulates a preexisting intellectual structure that contains all possible meanings. There is no room for the future to appear "in a different shape," as Anna puts the matter at one point (p. 473). *The Golden Notebook* is not this kind of unity: it is made up of contradictory strands of narration that seem to resolve into ontological levels but end up resisting strategies of naturalization, and it deals with the political perils of assuming that there is a coherent, explicable universe and a "real story" that adequately reflects it. It is full of gaps that leave room for subsequent developments and full of different kinds of writing that hint at techniques for realizing the future in a different shape, especially Lessing's own future productions in a variety of genres: space fiction, satire, allegory, apocalyptic, and—particularly with the Jane Somers novels of the early 1980s—fictional "diaries" that obstinately refuse to allow female experience to be absorbed into a transpersonal context—"little novels about the emotions."

I

"The point is," insists Anna at the opening of the first "Free Women" section, "the point is, that as far as I can see, everything's cracking

11Lessing, 1972 Preface to *The Golden Notebook* in the Bantam edition, p. x.

up" (p. 3). It is a point that the novel goes on to consider at some length, most evidently in its treatment of the failure of a single world view to encompass the whole of twentieth-century reality. Both Anna and her creator have a particular world view in mind, the orthodox Marxism of the mid-1950s that is thoroughly repudiated as Anna herself moves toward "crack-up" precisely because it fails to stand for "the whole person, the whole individual, striving to become as conscious and responsible as possible about everything in the universe" (p. 360). But the critique of ideology in this novel goes much further, beyond narrowly Marxist principles to the more general set of presuppositions governing Western culture in the modern period, ultimately addressing the assumption that any world view can be adequate, that reality is the sort of thing that can be held together as a unified whole.

This assumption was what Lessing had found most congenial in Marxist aesthetics and upheld in her 1957 essay "The Small Personal Voice," in which she made unity of vision the hallmark of the novels she termed "the highest point of literature," the classics of nineteenth-century realism. In this essay she explicitly identified realism with both metaphysical and moral coherence: the great writers of the period produced "art which springs so vigorously and naturally from a strongly-held, though not necessarily intellectually-defined, view of life that it absorbs symbolism" and had in common "a climate of ethical judgement; they shared certain values; they were humanists."[12] By the time she wrote *The Golden Notebook*, however, Lessing was publicly expressing her disaffection with both realism and the notion of an encompassing "view of life" that warrants the unequivocal sharing of "certain values."[13] Furthermore, she was linking unity of vision with the kind of unity of form that is an aesthetic requirement for the realist novel. Her aim, she said, was "to break a form; to break certain forms of consciousness and go beyond them,"[14] and both kinds of breakage—of form and of

[12]Lessing, "The Small Personal Voice," pp. 4–5.
[13]In the introduction to *Play with a Tiger* (London: Michael Joseph, 1962), for example, Lessing criticizes the premises of theatrical realism and elaborates the Laingian equation of "breakdown" with "break-through" that informs the "mad" scenes of *The Golden Notebook*.
[14]Letter from Lessing to her publishers, Michael Joseph, quoted on the dust jacket

consciousness—turned her away from the realist tradition. In turning away she committed herself to crack-up, fragmentation, and discontinuity to an extent that her critics are only beginning to acknowledge.[15] For despite a rhetoric of wholeness informing this encyclopedic novel, her emphasis throughout is on the complexity of experience, its intractability to integration, the difficulty of achieving coherence without inevitably succumbing to reduction. As a consequence, discontinuity achieves a significance that does not allow it to be simply subsumed under a "higher" unity: fragmentation, breakage, gaps, and lapses are precisely what allow possibility to emerge, on a number of levels. In effect, Lessing's theory and practice of fiction changed radically after "The Small Personal Voice," and *The Golden Notebook* assumes in the context of her later experiments the status of a transitional work, documenting her dissatisfaction with the conventions of not only nineteenth-century but also modernist fiction and mapping out directions for further and perhaps even more unsettling disruptions.

In *The Golden Notebook* her most obvious attack is on the coherence that realist fiction demands of characters, and the line she takes makes it clear that in the process she is throwing into question the assumptions behind most usual notions of identity. When Anna confronts her psychoanalyst (who has Jungian proclivities but a pointedly political name, Mrs Marks), she is challenging the rigid humanism that is the premise of both the realist novel and her own therapy:

> Look, if I'd said to you when I came in this afternoon: Yesterday I met a man at a party and I recognised in him the wolf, or the knight, or the monk, you'd nod and you'd smile. And we'd both feel the joy of recognition. But if I'd said: Yesterday I met a man at a party and suddenly he said something, and I thought: *Yes*, there's a hint of something—there's a crack in that man's personality like a gap in a dam, and through that gap the future might pour in a different shape—terrible perhaps, or marvellous, but something new—if I said that you'd frown. [p. 473]

---

of the British edition and cited by John L. Carey in "Art and Reality in *The Golden Notebook*," in *Doris Lessing: Critical Studies*, ed. Pratt and Dembo, p. 20.

[15]Important recent studies that acknowledge the "deconstructed" or "postmodern" structure of the novel are Sage, *Doris Lessing*; and Patrocinio P. Schweickart, "Reading a Wordless Statement: The Structure of Doris Lessing's *The Golden Notebook*," *Modern Fiction Studies* 31, no. 2 (1985), 263–79.

Under the premises of Anna's therapy the wolf, the knight, and the monk are archetypes, stock characters, finite in number, who together comprise all the possible human variations. In Mrs Marks's scheme of things, human nature is an unchanging essence that can manifest itself only in a fixed number of preexisting forms, so that recognition amounts to attaching the right label, assigning an individual to the proper category. The "joy of recognition" thus derives from the containing and controlling of possibility. Anna, on the other hand, anticipates kinds of people that elude classification because they elude containment; people who are, as she goes on to say, "cracked across" or "split" because "they are keeping themselves open for something." Earlier in the same conversation she had proposed that in the present age, possession of a coherent identity is damning evidence of limitation: "I've reached the stage where I look at people and say—he or she, they are whole at all because they've chosen to block off at this stage or that. People stay sane by blocking off, by limiting themselves" (p. 469). Unity, integrity, self-consistency, she implies, are not privileged, as they are in traditional therapy and traditional characterization. To be whole by present-day societal standards is not to have resisted fragmentation but to have been reduced to a single fragment.

If these passages most patently foreshadow the advent of a man (Saul Green in the notebooks, Milt in the "Free Women" narrative) who will accompany Anna through "breakdown" as a psychological experience, they also suggest that for the novelist the problem with conceiving character in terms of preexisting forms is that such forms do not allow "the future"—that is, anything genuinely new and unassimilated by the dominant culture—to be represented. Much of *The Golden Notebook* deals with questions of representation, particularly with the failure of "language" (a shorthand term that usually seems to refer to the conventions of traditional realist fiction) to reflect contemporary life, and Lessing's protagonists are most acutely aware of manipulating debased discursive counters when they are concerned with describing people. Ella reacts with fury to Mrs West's "disinfecting phrases, *lunatic fringe* and *career girls*," which reduce her most passionate commitment and her whole life-style to safe cliches (p. 177), and the notion that a unit of language has "disinfecting" properties recurs much later on, in one of Anna's childhood recollections, in which she remembers lying "awake, remembering everything in the day that had a quality of fear hidden in it; which might become part of a nightmare. I had to 'name' the frightening things, over and over, in a terrible litany; like a sort of disinfection by the conscious mind before I slept" (p. 616). "Language" here, as in the "naming" involved in Anna's therapy, is a means of making safe, of restricting to manageable dimensions, of ruling out the radically unknown. Similarly, after diagnosing Saul's "mother-trouble" in the jargon of mid-fifties pop psychoanalysis, Anna denounces both Saul and herself for accepting even provisionally a vocabulary of ready-made insights: "I'm naming you, Saul Green, and I'm naming you on such a low level that you ought to be angry. You should be ashamed, at the age of thirty-three, to be sitting there taking this kind of banal over-simplification from me" (p. 581). Use of such easy and accessible designations confirms the adage, a staple of both psychoanalytic and popular wisdom, that there is nothing new under the sun, and especially that humanity consists of a limited number of recurring variations on an eternal theme. If the idea is at root reassuring because it insists that no crisis, when properly understood, is unique, personal, or without precedent, it soothes at the expense of allowing development, as Anna points out to Molly in the opening scene of "Free Women": "[Mrs Marks] used to say, 'you're Electra,' or 'you're Antigone,' and that was the end, as far as she was concerned" (p. 5). But the novel that begins by raising the question of "the end" goes on to insist that "names" remain open-ended: the epithet "Free Women" does not "name" Anna and Molly definitively any more than the "Free Women" narrative constitutes the last word on the subject of who they are.

It is as a writer of fiction, specifically as a "blocked" writer who has previously produced one novel in the realist tradition, that Anna is most bothered by established conventions of "naming," which not only rule out surprises but seem to remove the truth of immediate experience beyond the reach of representation. In a Black notebook entry attempting to describe the man she calls Willi, she chooses the adjectives *Ruthless, Cold,* and *Sentimental* but also the adjectives *Kind, Warm,* and *Realistic* and concludes in frustration, "In describing any personality all these words are meaningless" (p. 71). Yet the problem is less that such words lack meaning than that they seem to mean too much, summing up a personality prematurely in a way that makes further predication not only incongruous but impossible. Anna's reminiscences about this man are shot through with moments of realization that she has categorized him out of existence—has excised his loneliness as inconsistent with his self-righteousness and predictability, for example. The value-laden language of everyday description presents a different but related difficulty: later in the same reflection she finds herself using the word *good* and comments, "Of course [such words] mean nothing, when you start to think about them. A good man, one says; a good woman; a nice man, a nice woman. Only in talk of course, these are not words you'd use in a novel. I'd be careful not to use them." The word *good*, unlike the descriptive terms Anna has used in trying to depict Willi, is too amorphous to be literary, implying an unspecified value system, on the one hand, and on the other hand, establishing nothing sufficiently "characteristic" to create identity in the novelistic terms she is used to. Yet *good* does have immediate application—it even seems to "name" a truth of a sort outside the boundaries of her writing—and she goes on to qualify the assertion that words of this kind "mean nothing": "Yet of that group, I will say simply, without further analysis, that George was a good person, and that Willi was not. . . . And furthermore, I'd bet that ten people picked at random off the street to meet them . . . would instantly agree with this classification—would, if I used the word *good*, simply like that, know what I meant" (p. 109). It is the context of a novel that appears to rob the word *good* of its significance, just as it is the requirement of producing a character in a literary work that rules out apparently contradictory adjectives. Early in the narrative Anna writes of her attempts to render her experience, "I am simply asking myself; Why a story at all . . . . Why not, simply, the truth?" (p. 63), and this opposition, story versus truth, haunts her as one meaning of her inability to write and as a paradigm of the tendency of preexisting form to "block off" possibility in the same way that people "block off" parts of themselves in order to stay whole. Although the novel was invented to represent both human personality and ethical touchstones for a culture—so much so that Anna appeals to the example of the nineteenth century novel in trying to convince Willi of the importance of George's bastard son

(p. 130)—she now believes that it "has been claimed by the disintegration and the collapse" (p. 110). It has reached a point in history where it stands in opposition to reality.

The notion that the truth has become alien to the forms originally created to express it is analogous to the notion, also pervasive in this novel, that history no longer admits of a Marxist interpretation. In both instances there is an apparent paradox: reality is incommensurate with realism; historical developments have rendered "the" historical viewpoint obsolete. In both instances the containing form—realism, Marxism—has become irrelevant because of a resistance on the part of the real, of history, to being contained, because of the phenomenon *The Golden Notebook* refers to variously as crackup, fragmentation, or chaos. And of course realism and Marxism are allied in Lessing's background as ideologies of containment. During the period chronicled by this novel Jack Lindsay was calling on contemporary writers to return to a "consciousness of unity of process which is adequate to deal with all aspects of life, social, artistic, scientific, yet see each aspect in relation to the whole," in other words, to embody a unified consciousness in a unified form.[16] But in *The Golden Notebook* Lessing chose to begin from a metafictionally split consciousness, by incorporating the dialogue about stories and truth into what is after all a story, using the established form to comment on its own limits, and went on to remake form to accommodate the "cracked" and "split" characters she was interested in depicting. To a great extent the requirements of characterization are given responsibility for wrenching the fictional discourse away from realism. As Anna tells a skeptical Mrs Marks, "I'm convinced that there are whole areas of me made by the kind of experience women haven't had before" (p. 471), and as a writer she is most interested in rendering the woman who is the product of this kind of experience. But she is up against a concept of identity formed and enforced by the literature that she herself (and Lessing herself) has espoused and helped produce; against "language" as guardian and guarantor of a humanism that perceives humanity as unchanging and that has in turn become rigid and conservative.

[16]Jack Lindsay, *After the Thirties*, p. 84. Jenny Taylor also quotes this passage in "Situating Reading," p. 29.

An apparently unlikely ally, Philippe Sollers, theorist and practitioner of the *nouveau roman*, has written in similar terms about this sort of "language," which has created an apparently inescapable definition of identity and which requires another sort of language entirely (his own critical prose here plays on the attempt to transcend itself) to evade it:

> Everything happens as though these books were henceforth written in advance: as if they were part of this all-powerful, anonymous language and thought which reign inside and outside, from public information to the mutest intimacy, with an exaggerated visibility which renders them invisible. Our *identity* depends on it: what is thought of us, what we think of ourselves, and the way our life is insensibly arranged. In oneself, one recognizes only a character from a novel. (In me, speaking to you, you recognize only a character from a novel.) What language would escape this insidious, incessant language which always seems to be there before we think of it?[17]

The notion of identity sustained by "this all-powerful, anonymous language" rules out certain possible characters. In the terms Lessing proposes, it rules out the possibility that certain people can be written as characters, as Anna discovers when she tries to evoke the African leader Tom Mathlong by "naming" him:

> I tried to make him stand in my room, a courteous, ironical figure, but I failed. I told myself I had failed because this figure, unlike all the others, had a quality of detachment. He was the man who performed actions, played roles, that he believed to be necessary for the good of others, even while he preserved an ironic doubt about the results of his actions. It seemed to me that this particular kind of detachment was something we needed very badly in this time, but that very few people had it, and it was certainly a long way from me. [p. 597]

What Anna is discovering is that the old methods of "naming" are insufficient. In the course of the narratives in the Blue and Golden notebooks she learns how to go back over her experiences and " 'name' them in a different way" (p. 616) in order to learn how to represent such a character, "cracked" or "split" in his "quality of

---

[17]Philippe Sollers, "The Novel and the Experience of Limits," in *Surfiction: Fiction Now and Tomorrow*, 2d ed., ed. Raymond Federman (Chicago: Swallow Press, 1981), p. 61.

detachment" and needed "very badly in this time." Mr Mathlong, barely sketched in this passage, is in fact a "different shape" for the future in several different senses—looking forward, for instance, to the cosmic disinterestedness of Klorathy in the *Canopus in Argos* series.

That the time requires new kinds of people is most evident early in the account of Ella, the protagonist of Anna's fragmentary novel-in-process. Also a writer, Ella is composing the story of a character who discovers himself in the act of committing suicide and realizes that this act is implicit in the continuity of his life. Writing out of a barely acknowledged sense of her own dead-endedness, in both her life and her art, she reflects on her affinity with this situation: "I would find myself just about to jump out of an open window or turning on the gas in a small closed-in room, and I would say to myself, without any emotion, but rather with the sense of suddenly understanding something I should have understood long before: Good Lord! So that's what I've been meaning to do. That's been it all the time!" (p. 174). The plot is strikingly similar to that of Lessing's own 1958 short story "To Room Nineteen," in which a well-off, conventionally happy matron finds suicide in a continuum with all the other actions stemming from a life that has "nothing wrong" with it, while an ironically omniscient narrator contributes a running commentary underscoring the absence of alternatives.[18] In both works the closure implied in traditional notions of character is deadly, and in both the suicide seems the inevitable culmination of a linear plot that works itself out so economically that the end is implicit in the beginning. The example of these stories suggests that in the absence of a gap through which the future can flow in a different shape, there can be no future.

Ella herself seems not only to arrive at this conclusion but to recognize the danger inherent in the fact that she is the protagonist of a traditional novel, for as she develops she begins to elude the Jungian theme of doubling that Anna has set out for her in the "theme or motif" of *The Shadow of the Third* (pp. 206–7) and begins to contemplate writing about the topic that Anna herself had set

---

[18]Doris Lessing, "To Room Nineteen," *Stories* (New York: Vintage, 1978), pp. 396–428.

against the Jungian archetypalism of Mrs Marks: "Perhaps next time I'll try to write about that—people who deliberately try to be something else, try to break their own form as it were" (p. 466). In her last appearance in the novel, shortly before the Yellow notebook itself "breaks down" into fragmentary metanarratives—ideas for short stories, parodies of contemporary modes of writing—Ella outlines the plot of an episode that eerily foreshadows the ensuing affair between Anna and Saul while in effect reversing the whole imbedding structure by suggesting that she is the author, Anna the character she has created: "I've got to accept the patterns of self-knowledge which mean unhappiness or at least a dryness. But I can twist it into victory. A man and a woman—yes. Both at the end of their tether. Both cracking up because of a deliberate attempt to transcend their own limits. And out of the chaos, a new kind of strength" (p. 467). For the characters in the story whom Ella seems determined to find by looking "inwards," crack-up and chaos are preconditions for novelty and in fact are required if such characters are to transcend their limits. But the notation is also self-reflexive, pointing to the sense in which Ella herself is implicated in the breaking of form, as a deliberate attempt on the part of Anna "to be something else . . . to break [her] own form as it were."

II

If on the metafictional level of writing *about* writing Lessing loads her discourse with statements of intent to break form, the characters she has created to populate the worlds of the novel in effect act out the dilemma of characterization that Anna has proposed, either achieving coherence by "blocking off" to the point where they become virtual caricatures—custom-ridden like Richard, monsters of denial like Nelson or DeSilva, emotionally leucotomized like Cy Maitland, literally mutilated like Tommy in the "Free Women" narrative—or, alternatively, so "cracked" and "split" that existing conventions seem wholly inadequate to portray them. The caricatured figures are overwhelmingly male. They tend to body forth professional, national, and sexual stereotypes and can be adequately "named" in a few well-chosen phrases. Richard, for instance, is first introduced with a negation: despite appearances, Anna tells Molly, he should not be understood as "an enterprising little businessman, like a jumped-up grocer" (p. 24). The joke is that this is precisely what he is; his vast financial holdings and considerable power only make him more rather than less of a petit bourgeois, whose banal and predictable self-justification, "I preserve the forms" (p. 26), indicates the extent to which he himself is preformed and unchanging.

Richard's "blocked off" nature is revealed early in the "Free Women" narrative through his assumption that physical and emotional aspects of a personal relationship can be distinguished. Throughout the narrative this sexual version of the mind/body problem is associated with men—as Molly expostulates, "At least [women have] more sense than to use words like physical and emotional as if they didn't connect" (p. 31)—and suggests that the female perspective is at least relatively more encompassing than the male perspective.[19] If Richard is the English version of the emotionally flattened male, strangely impotent in his power and promiscuity, his transatlantic equivalent is Nelson, the Canadian whose flamboyant behavior is associated (at least by the English) both with North Americans and with show business and who combines political acumen with a profound and wholly unacknowledged misogyny. Their Third World counterpart, the Ceylonese De Silva, is the Europeanized intellectual who has divorced the physical from the emotional to the point where he could pass as a textbook example of sadism. A slight variation on this type is Cy Maitland, the stock American

[19]It does not, however, suggest that women are morally superior to men, as is implied by Milt's sentimental (and self-serving) assertion near the close of "Free Women" that women are "tougher . . . kinder . . . in a position to take it" (p. 663). Gayle Greene points out that *The Golden Notebook* articulates an apparent paradox, that "contemporary society is 'worse for' men than for women, leaving them damaged, divided, dehumanized" ("Women and Men in Doris Lessing's *Golden Notebook*: Divided Selves," in *The (M)other Tongue: Essays in Feminist Psychoanalytic Interpretation*, ed. Shirley Nelson Garner, Claire Kahane and Madelon Sprengnether [Ithaca: Cornell University Press, 1985], p. 280). As Lessing indicates, men have both power and privilege in this society, and it is precisely these advantages that prove damaging and limiting. Adrienne Rich sums up the situation in *Of Woman Born: Motherhood as Experience and Institution* (New York: Bantam, 1976), p. 49: "To hold power over others means that the powerful is permitted a kind of short-cut through the complexity of human personality. He does not have to enter intuitively into the souls of the powerless, or to hear what they are saying in their many languages, including the language of silence. Colonialism exists by virtue of this short-cut—how else could so few live among so many and understand so little?"

from a Wyoming that never was, whom Ella services out of liking and self-denigration, the latter motive implied by the one trait the two of them have in common, indifference to the prospect of being killed (pp. 317–18). Cy both caps the other stereotypes and glosses them. "They talked about his work. He specialised in leucotomies: 'Boy, I've cut literally hundreds of brains in half!' " (p. 328) The flat, factual tone of this passage, along with the boyish bravura and complete absence of self-irony in the exclamation, are indexes of how cut in half Cy himself is, and of how little of his professional competence is reflected on the personal level. Ella encapsulates the defining feature of all these men when "she thinks for the hundredth time that in their emotional life all these intelligent men use a level so much lower than anything they use for work, that they might be different creatures" (p. 457).

Tommy, the son of Molly and Richard, is perhaps the most developed of the stereotyped figures: developed in that he is represented as *becoming* a parody of the self-limited human being, in a particularly grisly and symbolic manner. Confronted at the beginning of "Free Women" with a comparatively unrestricted choice of life, in effect a choice of possible people to be, he is presented in that narrative as sliding into suicide with the same inevitability as the protagonist of Ella's novel. He succeeds only in blinding himself, and this denouement turns into a solution to the problem of seeing too many alternatives. With his vision thus restricted, he first becomes "political" in a way that virtually parodies his mother's life of activism, and at the conclusion is settling into his father's role as a captain of industry, his blindness so intrinsic to what he has turned into that it is no longer mentioned. Molly articulates the paradox of his mutilation shortly after his return from the hospital, "He's happy for the first time in his life. . . . he's all in one piece for the first time in his life" (p. 378), and Tommy's backward metamorphosis from a complex and deeply engaged young man to a single-minded and therefore coherent personality constitutes a fable pointing up how other characters are also self-maimed, self-blinded.[20]

[20]Elizabeth Abel views the Tommy of "Free Women" as Anna's own "dark double, who confronts the same tormenting existential questions, vehemently denies that he is going through a 'phase' that differentiates his point of view from hers, and, on the brink of plunging into the same chaos she faces, chooses the alternative route of

Such stereotyped characters are exactly equivalent to the verbal cliches that define them; they are circumscribed by the "disinfecting phrases" of popular wisdom and psychoanalysis, "named" to the point of sterility in terms of professional, national, and especially sexual identity. They are only extreme versions, however, of a tendency to use self-definition as a means of closing off possibility that occurs in all the characters, including Anna and Ella. Both protagonists, in fact, allow themselves to be constrained by a word that, like *good* in Anna's meditation on literary language, is deeply ambiguous yet apparently meaningful. The word is *real*, and the two women use it primarily to intensify gender categories, as in a "real woman," a "real man," without being able to control the ways in which the word ultimately qualifies and narrows these categories. Like *good*, *real* has meaning: it "names" something that most people would claim to be able to recognize, although most people would not be able to explain how they recognize it. Like *good*, it also privileges one group of people over another, and such privileging is always political. Anna and Ella use the term in a variety of contexts and in a variety of tones ranging from affirmation to irony, but despite their consciousness and caution, they cannot evade the affinity between the essentialism of this *real* and the constriction of the realism that as writers they—and, of course, Lessing herself—want to renounce.[21]

---

blindness as the limitation that preserves control" ("(E)merging Identities: The Dynamics of Female Friendship in Contemporary Fiction by Women," *Signs: Journal of Women in Culture and Society* 6, no. 3 [1981], 431). Roberta Rubenstein similarly argues for Tommy as projected "inner critic" in *The Novelistic Vision of Doris Lessing: Breaking the Forms of Consciousness* (Urbana: University of Illinois Press, 1979), pp. 103–4. The third and fourth sections of this chapter examine the notion of projection and some implications of the novel's structure: this analysis complicates, although it in no way discredits, Abel's and Rubenstein's arguments.

[21]In an important and relatively early article, "Alienation of the Woman Writer in *The Golden Notebook*" (reprinted in *Doris Lessing: Critical Studies*, pp. 54–63), Ellen Morgan maintains that Lessing uses *real* unironically and that this usage is a manifestation of her own biologism, an aspect of authorial self-division explicable in light of the presuppositions about women and sex roles current in the early 1960s: "The woman writer in this situation is unlikely to conceive of the relative status of women and men in political terms; prevailing opinion convinces her that the condition of women in society is rooted in biological and psychological immutables. She may, nevertheless, be acutely sensitive to and resentful of the power dynamics which characterize female-male relations" (pp. 62–63). Elaine Showalter, in *A Literature of Their Own: British Women Novelists From Brontë to Lessing* (Princeton: Princeton Uni-

The "real woman" is first heralded by Mrs Marks, who uses the phrase to explain and approve of why Anna's sexual response to her lover Michael is contingent on how he accepts her. Anna observes, "She uses this word, a woman, a real woman, exactly as she does artist, a true artist. An absolute," and her reaction is to laugh (p. 237), although the analogy recalls an earlier, angrier passage in which the psychoanalyst invoked the cliche of the "true artist" as a sort of cosmic justification for shortcoming. In that episode, Mrs Marks tried to excuse what Anna perceived as impotence and sterility by appealing to the maxim "the artist writes out of an incapacity to live," and Anna noted a willingness to utter "commonplaces in her capacity as witch-doctor she would have been ashamed of if she were with friends and not in the consulting room" and went on to denounce the compartmentalization this retreat into banality implied: "One level for life, another for the couch. I couldn't stand it; that is, ultimately, what I couldn't stand. Because it means one level of morality for life, and another for the sick" (p. 62). The absolute status of "real woman" in the therapeutic context seems another instance of this principle, at least inasmuch as it purports to vindicate a debilitating level of emotional dependence and passivity. Yet in spite of a generally skeptical attitude toward essentialism and compartmentalization, both Anna and Ella cling to this notion of the "real woman," even on occasions when its limitations are clearly exposed.

For example, writing of the affair between Ella and Paul, which in many ways mirrors the affair between Anna and Michael, Anna observes,

> Any intelligent person could have foreseen the end of this affair from its beginning. And yet I, Anna, like Ella with Paul, refused to see it. Paul gave birth to Ella, the naïve Ella. He destroyed in her the knowing, doubting, sophisticated Ella and again and again he put her intelligence to sleep, and with her willing connivance, so that she floated darkly on her love for him, on her naivety, which is another word for a spontaneous creative faith. [p. 211]

---

versity Press, 1977); and Diana Trilling, in the *Times Literary Supplement*, 13 October 1978, 1165, make similar arguments. Gayle Greene points out, however, that "neither critic makes any distinction between Lessing and her protagonist" ("Women and Men," p. 294 n. 28). This discussion develops from Greene's observation.

If this passage expresses Anna's desire for an experience that is not, like Ella's story of the suicide, structured in an inevitable progression so that the end is implicit in the beginning, it also suggests that destroying "the knowing, doubting, sophisticated" self, or allowing a man to put one's "intelligence to sleep" amounts to a mutilation as catastrophic as Tommy's self-blinding. That this willed naïvety is tantamount to stupidity occurs to Anna when she describes, again after the fact, the climax of her abortive affair with Nelson: "Sometimes I dislike women, I dislike us all, because of our capacity for not-thinking when it suits us; we choose not to think when we are reaching out for happiness" (p. 485). But such perceptions are more often engulfed by nostalgia for a sort of sexual golden age, in which traditionally feminine dependency is written into the social structure. Thus Ella muses: "What is terrible is that after every one of the phases of my life is finished, I am left with no more than some banal commonplace that everyone knows: in this case, that women's emotions are all still fitted for a kind of society that no longer exists. My deep emotions, my real ones, are to do with my relationship with a man. One man. But I don't live that kind of life, and I know few women who do (p. 314). Her meditation is peculiarly ahistorical, as the Marxist Anna, if not the politically innocent Ella, presumably knows: while past societies have frequently prescribed monogamy for women (or at least for women of certain classes) they have never required reciprocity from men. The "kind of society that no longer exists" in which a woman has a "relationship with a man. One man" is in fact the kind of society inhabited in the fictional present by such women as Marion, Muriel Tanner, and Nelson's unnamed wife, that is, a society in which the woman has a "relationship" and the man has outside affairs and uses her as a source for everything from mothering to a clean shirt.[22] Furthermore, that Ella locates her "real emotions" in a hazily ideal-

---

[22]The Anna Freeman of *Play with a Tiger* (in *The Golden Notebook*, p. 471, Freeman is Anna Wulf's maiden name) is confronted with precisely this role and expressly rejects it. For an excellent discussion of the relation of the two plays to *The Golden Notebook*, see Paul Schlueter, *The Novels of Doris Lessing* (Carbondale, Ill: Southern Illinois University Press, 1973), pp. 77–84.

ized past is another indication that the word *real* is too restrictive to be meaningful in a contemporary context: paradoxically, it falls short of "naming" present reality.

The "real woman" 's counterpart, the "real man," is also a relic of the past, although he is dying out far more rapidly; as Anna notes, "Women have this deep instinctive need to build a man up as a man. . . . I suppose this is because real men become fewer and fewer, and we are frightened, trying to create men" (p. 484). He is never positively characterized, remaining equivocally defined by his contrast with "sexual cripples" (p. 484) on one hand and male homosexuals on the other: defined, that is, as someone who is both capable of and interested in heterosexual intercourse. He is not necessarily, however, someone who either likes or respects women, and consequently the value attached to his "real" status is gradually drawn into question. In "Free Women," for instance, Anna, reflecting on the relationship between her homosexual lodger Ivor and her daughter Janet, asks herself, "What do I mean when I say he's not a man? . . . I know that with 'a real man' there would be a whole area of tension, of wry understanding that there can't be with Ivor; there would be a whole dimension there isn't now; and yet he's charming with her, and so what do I mean by 'A real man'?" (p. 391). The ironizing quotation marks suggest the extent of her doubt. The "real man" has been conceived as so inherently other than the self-abasing "real woman" that his polarization is manifested as misogyny, as Anna finally realizes, listening to the calculated derision of Ivor and his lover Ronnie: "The mockery, the defence of the homosexual, was nothing more than the polite over-gallantry of a 'real' man, the 'normal' man who intends to set bounds to his relationship with a woman, consciously or not. Usually unconsciously. It was the same cold evasive emotion, taken a step further; there was a difference in degree but not in kind" (p. 393). In this passage *real* is aligned with *normal*, a term already suspect because of its association with the evaluative labels of psychoanalysis. In a situation where Anna was exercising her critical facility, the "normal" man would be the man who is fatally blocked, hemmed in, circumscribed. It is thus the start of a reversion to conventionality—conscious, ironic reversion, but reversion nonetheless—when the Anna of "Free Women" vows, "By God, there are a few real men left, and I'm going to see

[Janet] gets one of them. I'm going to see she grows up to recognise a real man when she meets one" (p. 404), for the examples of recognizable "real men" that Lessing has provided within the novel offer women little potential for relationships. Perhaps the purest specimen is George Hounslow of the African reminiscences, the man who was identified as "good" in contradistinction to Willi. He is described as a throwback because he is "a man who really, very much, needed women," but this need has specific dimensions: "George needed a woman to submit to him, he needed a woman to be under his spell physically. . . . When George looked at a woman he was imagining her as she would be when he had fucked her into insensibility" (p. 124). In line with this characterization he is a philanderer, as forthrightly polygamous as Anna and Ella are monogamous; as he tells the young Anna, "I could take you to bed now—and then Marie, that's my black girl, and then go back to my wife tonight and have her, and be happy with all three of you. Do you understand that, Anna?" She reports responding " 'No' . . . lying on behalf of all women, and thinking of his wife, who made me feel caged" (p. 133). In this confrontation the "real man" and the "real woman" are at a standoff. Both are thwarted by normality, hemmed in by the restrictions implicit in the qualification *real*, and prevented in particular from having any contact with each other.

The lure of the "normal" also affects Ella, who tries to interpret the period of deprivation after Paul has left by imaginatively looking back on it, in the process construing it as a completed action, over and done with, a story. She assures herself that "when she loved a man again, she would return to normal: a woman, that is, whose sexuality would ebb and flow in response to his. A woman's sexuality is, so to speak, contained by a man, if he is a real man; she is, in a sense, put to sleep by him, she does not think about sex" (p. 455). This version of normality is an article of faith for her, although she does remark "How strange that one should hold on to a set of sentences, and have faith in them" (p. 455), effectively making into dogma the requirement of having one's "sexuality . . . , so to speak, contained by a man." When this credo is transposed to the level of Anna's own experience, however, it crumbles under the pressure of its internal contradictions, just before Anna herself crumbles, in the aftermath of the "deadly" night she spends with De Silva. During that night, finding herself as "cool, detached, abstracted" as her partner, she reflexively turns to a "set of sentences." "For I kept thinking stubbornly: Of course it's him, not me. For men create these things, they create us." But for the first time this attempt to pass on responsibility for her emotional state strikes her as unsatisfactory. "In the morning, remembering how I clung, how I always cling to this, I felt foolish. Because why should it be true?" (p. 501). The question becomes a preamble to the experience of "madness" that she shares with Saul Green, and it implies the condition that makes this experience liberating as well as devastating: Anna *chooses* to enter into Saul's breakdown, to participate in his anxiety state, and even, it seems, to fall in love with him in the first place. She can accordingly be "contained" by him in a way that is freeing rather than inhibiting because containment is her option, an option that she can, and does, terminate when necessary.[23]

The essentialist, rather Lawrentian notion of the "real" man and woman must yield if people are to "try to be something else, to break their own form as it were."[24] Anna works through the concept of the sex-coded "real" at the same time as she works through the concept of a stable, "real" self. With Saul in the Blue and Golden notebooks she enacts parodic versions of traditional female roles: the jealous, vindictive woman scorned; the mewing, helpless victim ("Oh boohoo, and my dainty pink-tipped forefinger pointed at my

[23]In the Blue notebook she reports "lying in bed examining the phrase 'in love' as if it were the name of a disease I could choose not to have" (p. 558). Later she tells herself, "Well, I'll never suffer from my own anxiety state, so I might just as well experience someone else's while I get the chance" (p. 575). And she exerts control by denying it when she tells Saul, "You're going to have to break it. I ought to, but I'm not strong enough," inserting her lucidity into their temporary structure of interdependence: "Anyway, you'll go by yourself when Janet comes back" (p. 621).

[24]Elizabeth Wilson notes, "The Lawrentian ideal of relationships between men and women was influential in Britain in radical circles in the late 1950s and early 1960s" ("Rereading Lessing and de Beauvoir" in *Notebooks/Memoirs/Archives*, ed. Taylor, p. 68), and Nicole Ward Jouve observes aspects of " 'Lawrentian' fulfillment" in the subsequent *Landlocked* ("Of Mud and Other Matter—*The Children of Violence*," in *Notebooks/Memoirs/Archives*, ed. Taylor, p. 79), but it seems reasonable to assume that Lessing was no less critical of "Lawrentian" influences than she was of Jungian or Marxist ones.

white, pink-tipped betrayed bosom" [p. 630]); the suffocating mother. And in a final climactic night she plays out with him "every man-woman role imaginable," feeling "condemned to play them now because I had refused them in life" (p. 604). But in another sense this overriding of the "real" as an absolute value, along with the transcending of other categories that restrict human potential to the definable limits of "character," has already occurred, indeed, is the structural premise of the novel as a whole. For Anna is already "cracked" or "split" into more than one character, most obviously in the persona of Ella, whose experiences tend to figure as no more "fictional" than Anna's own because the four notebooks are always presented as equivalent, as on a single ontological level, more radically as the novel develops and the accounts of Anna's life in "Free Women" and in the various "factual" notebooks become more and more divergent, giving rise to two distinct Annas who can be neither reduced nor subordinated to one another.

III

If one aspect of Anna's "splitting" is the character Ella, Ella's development serves to indicate how ambiguous the notions of "splitting"—and of character—can be. Initially presented as Anna's fictional creation, Ella soon emerges as a version of Anna, a double or second self who both replicates certain of Anna's experiences and adds new material that Anna has presumably suppressed from other notebooks. She thus appears to be a projection in the relatively straightforward sense of a mirror image, a different angle on Anna, and her name, with its similarly doubled central letter and final *a*, suggests that she is a variation on the essential Anna, a product of simple and easily decoded substitutions.

But Anna's sketch of the "main theme, or motif" of *The Shadow of the Third* complicates this construction of the relation between creator and character by introducing a psychoanalytical concept of projection that superadds desire and fear to the notion of the double. Within *The Shadow of the Third*, as Anna delineates the plot, Ella is to become increasingly obsessed with the image of "a serene, calm, unjealous, unenvious, undemanding woman, full of resources of happiness inside herself, self-sufficient, yet always ready to give happiness when it is asked for"—precisely the "real woman" in her most idealized form—and eventually to recognize this woman as her own shadow, everything she is not but wants most to be (p. 27).[25] Jungian therapy provides the theoretical basis for regarding such an apparently alien figure as potentially integral to the self, and for denominating the two selves in a dialectic of values: Ella thinks, "I have as a shadow a good woman, grown-up and strong and unasking. Which means that I am using with [Paul] my 'negative' self," and she then identifies the "third" of her obsession as her "positive" or "good" self (p. 20). In some ways, at least, Ella is also Anna's projection in this second sense, the reversed, wholly other self of desire, as Anna comments near the end of the Golden notebook when she calls Ella back into being: "After a while I realised I was doing what I had done before, creating 'the third'—the woman altogether better than I was" (p. 637). Ella in this passage represents the "good" Anna, but in earlier sections of the Yellow notebook she is the dependent, demanding woman who reacts with rage and despair to the conventions of sexual manipulation, an incipient "bad" Anna whom Anna fears and uses the notebooks to control.[26]

Even if Ella is nothing but a projection of Anna, then, her relation to her original may still be shifty, inverted, difficult to recuperate. The correspondence may be positive, in which case revelations about Ella apply directly to Anna, or negative, in which case revelations about Ella apply inversely to Anna, describing what she is not but desires to be or fears becoming. But the project of reading Ella as a source of information about Anna is further complicated by the fact that the whole notion of

[25]Ellen Morgan notes that this woman functions as both a stereotype and a symbol of invulnerability to male-inflicted pain ("Alienation of the Woman Writer," p. 59).

[26]Ella is more representative than Anna. As Sydney Janet Kaplan observes in *Feminine Consciousness in the Modern British Novel* (Urbana: University of Illinois Press, 1975), "Ella . . . is revealed as tending more toward the conventional and the general than Anna. She is both more passive than the Anna of the blue notebook and more stereotyped. Her utterances echo sentiments from a popularized version of the psychology of sex that often sound just like the writing in the women's magazines Ella works for. The style of the yellow notebook is thus much cruder—and more incomplete—than in the others" (p. 155).

character as authorial projection presumes a theory of writing as unmediated self-expression, and presumes in addition an unproblematic distinction between fictional "fact" and fictional "fiction." Anna herself dismisses the self-expression theory, once again citing the intervention of preexisting forms, of the categories of a novel or a story, as evidence against the equation of the artist with her production: "I see Ella, walking slowly about a big room, thinking, waiting. I, Anna, see Ella. Who is, of course, Anna. But that is the point, for she is not. The moment I, Anna, write: Ella rings up Julia to announce, etc., then Ella floats away from me and becomes someone else. I don't understand what happens at the moment Ella separates herself from me and becomes Ella. No one does. It's enough to call her Ella, instead of Anna" (p. 459). By making Ella external, other than herself, Anna admits the possibility that other people may also serve as models for representation. "Why did I choose the name Ella?" she muses and launches into an anecdote about an Ella she met at a party, an anecdote especially disconcerting at this point in the narrative because the identification of the two characters has never before been seriously questioned. "Well, I would never do that," she concludes. "That's not Anna at all"—and goes on to incorporate the tied-back straight hair and the white, beautiful hands of this "real" Ella into the physical description of her erstwhile persona (p. 460), a move clearly implying that precisely because of the mimesis central to realist characterization there are respects in which Ella is not any sort of version of Anna. Furthermore, because she has invented not simply a fantasized self but a character, Anna sets in motion a system of conventions dictating an internal logic to Ella's behavior. Ella must act "in character," a requirement that rules out certain aspects of projection. In the passage that acknowledges Ella as Anna's "third," for example, Anna goes on to withdraw the identification, for Ella could not be so morally superior without violating her own coherence. The terms in which Anna couches this judgment, moreover, are fairly startling in their suggestion of how unstable the distinction between "real" and "fictional" character has become at this point, for in describing her own creation she identifies literary convention and nature, realism and reality: "For I could positively mark

the point where Ella *left reality,* left how she would, *in fact,* behave because of *her nature;* and move into a larger generosity of
personality impossible to her" (p. 637, my emphasis). If the restrictions embodied in the literary tradition Anna is trying to
evade seem here to have infiltrated the real world, seem to have
become reified as natures impossible to transcend or transgress, it
is equally true that the wording of this statement makes Ella as
real, or as fictional, as Anna. The demands of realist characterization have granted Ella an autonomy that makes her resist naturalization as a "fictional" character within the dominant fiction.

The theory that Ella is a projection of Anna assumes that Ella's
function in the novel is to reveal more about Anna, that Ella's story,
correctly interpreted, augments and completes Anna's story. Together the Ella and Anna narratives should add up to a "whole
person" and a "real story." But this adding up involves reconstruing
"fiction" (about Ella) as "fact" (about Anna), and demands that
"fictionalized" characters and incidents be rigorously subordinated:
for instance, Paul Tanner is not "real" but Michael is; Cy Maitland
is not "real" but De Silva is. Keeping the subordinations straight is
surprisingly difficult, because even though there are stylistic mark-
ers—such as the retrospective commentary interpolated after a reported event ("Later he would say," "But it was only later she would
use a phrase like")—which differentiate the discourse of the Yellow
notebook from entries in the Black, Red, and Blue notebooks, such
techniques do not signal which narrative is the imbedded one. As
a consequence Anna's and Ella's stories invite comparison with,
rather than reduction to, one another. Paul Tanner and Michael are
clearly similar kinds of men from very different backgrounds (although the "fictional" Paul is far more fully realized than the "real"
Michael), and Cy Maitland and De Silva are in their different ways
equally mutilated, or equally caricatures. For the same sort of reasons, it is often hard to naturalize Ella's experiences as Anna's inventions or projections. Ella's life seems as detailed, as absorbing,
and ultimately as important as Anna's.

This last observation seems especially incongruous in view of the
notion that Ella represents a "splitting" of Anna. "Splitting" as a
strategy ought to diminish character. Following this logic, one critic
has surmised that in the Yellow notebook Anna projects herself as

both Ella and Paul, who take up, respectively, the romantic and the political aspects of her personality.[27] Yet Ella is more than a partial Anna, and paradoxically, her apparent lack of sophistication—she has never been affiliated with the Communist party, never been to South Africa, never been in therapy—allows something new to emerge through her narrative: a concern with overtly feminist issues, as distinct from issues of class, race, and the collective human psyche. In the Ella narrative Lessing has omitted those intellectual categories that absorb the events of Anna's life into a theoretical hierarchy. In the process she has omitted a number of the categories that trivialize Anna's experiences as a woman.

The Marxist and Freudian-Jungian explanatory systems are the preexisting forms that Anna has criticized as preventing the radically new from making an appearance. Yet Anna allows her tenuous allegiance to these systems to mute some of the most significant aspects of her own experience, as if communism and psychoanalysis were in charge of "what's real" and could rule out "the emotions," the subject matter of what Molly scornfully termed "little novels"— by implication, of course, "women's writing." One of the most dramatic instances of such muting is the long entry in the Blue notebook in which Anna tries to record without conscious editing the events of a single day, in hopes of approaching "the truth" that obstinately eludes the discourse of a novel or a story. Lessing ironizes this project at the outset by making the day that Anna selects hardly a "normal" one, despite Anna's desperate attempt after the initial writing to neutralize the most alarming implications (p. 368). In the course of this day she decides to leave the Communist party and is left, for good, by her lover of the past five years. Running along underneath the recounting of these two terminations, however, is a third theme of her reaction to her menstrual period, a hitherto invisible fact of her experience, which emerges with the deliberate attempt to "be conscious." She describes her period, without apparent awareness of contradiction, as "an entrance into an emotional state, recurring regularly, that is of no particular importance" (p. 340); what assumes great importance in this account is her re-

[27]Betsy Draine, *Substance under Pressure: Artistic Coherence and Evolving Form in the Novels of Doris Lessing* (Madison: University of Wisconsin Press, 1983), p. 79.

vulsion toward her own reproductive capacities and by extension toward her sexual identity. In the course of a day spent among men or anticipating the arrival of a man, she is constantly darting into bathrooms to wash between her legs, "conscious of the possibility of bad smells" (p. 340). She does not connect this evidence of self-loathing with the failure of her power struggle with the overbearing John Butte or the breakdown of communications with Jack, her best friend within the party, nor does she interpret it in light of her passive attendance on Michael and her acceptance of his complete control over their affair. She does not interpret it at all, in fact; it does not count as datum even though it has emerged with stark clarity from the experiment in getting at "the truth," for within the cultural contexts of both the party and "personal relationships," misogyny is a governing assumption. In the same way, and in the same section, she dismisses female guilt as "irrational," "impersonal," and "a habit of the nerves from the past" (p. 365) and female anger at male privilege as "resentment against injustice, an impersonal poison" (p. 333), without in either case construing the impersonality she notes as an index of political significance. "Long ago, in the course of the sessions with [Mrs Marks], I learned that the resentment, the anger, is impersonal," she writes. "It is the disease of women in our time. I can see it in women's faces, their voices, every day, or in the letters that come into the office" (p. 333). But the Marxism she is familiar with does not "name" the situation of women as oppression, and the psychoanalytic tradition encourages her to classify female oppression as pathology, "the disease of women in our time," a phrase that reduces the phenomenon to beneath consideration.

In particular, Ella and Anna differ in the degree of their involvement with the condition that Betty Friedan, in a ground-breaking study published in the year following the publication of *The Golden Notebook*, was to call "the problem that has no name."[28] Significantly, Anna encounters the problem in the course of canvassing for Communist party candidates:

> Five lonely women going mad quietly by themselves, in spite of husband and children or rather because of them. The quality they all had:

[28]Betty Friedan, *The Feminine Mystique* (New York: Norton, 1963).

self-doubt. A guilt because they were not happy. The phrase they all used: "There must be something wrong with me." Back in the campaign H.Q. I mentioned these women to the woman in charge for the afternoon. She said: "Yes, whenever I go canvassing, I get the heeby-jeebies. This country's full of women going mad all by themselves." A pause, then she added, with a slight aggressiveness, the other side of the self-doubt, the guilt shown by the women I'd talked to: "Well, I used to be the same until I joined the Party and got myself a purpose in life." I've been thinking about this—the truth is, these women interest me more than the election campaign. [p. 167]

In *The Feminine Mystique* Friedan documented the same "going mad . . . in spite of husband and children or rather because of them," the same overwhelming sense of futility coupled with self-doubt and guilt, among a large cross section of middle-class American housewives, and her analysis became a cornerstone of the ensuing women's liberation movement. Anna, however, cannot fit her interest in "these women" into the traditionally political context of the Red notebook and finds their situation equally irrelevant to the focuses of the Black and Blue notebooks. In effect, she adopts the strategy of the party organizer, who, as she astutely notes, is displaying the same guilt reactions as the "women going mad all by themselves," substituting party busy-ness for reflection on what such mass discontent may imply for her own life. She relegates "the problem that has no name" to the realm of the fictional, to the Yellow notebook, which begins barely two pages after this entry.

This first Yellow notebook section introduces Ella by placing her in an environment of specifically female concerns. Like Lessing's later protagonist Jane Somers, Ella works for a women's magazine, and it is in this capacity that she has become interested in the situation of the women her employer's wife indelicately terms the "lunatic fringe," the working-class housewives who write to the magazine's medical column about their pervasive unhappiness. It is in this capacity also that she becomes involved with Paul Tanner, a psychiatrist from a working-class background who is sympathetic to these women; later sections add the compromising information that he may well be married to one of them. The possibility that Paul is on such an overt level an accomplice in oppression is one of the many factors undercutting his authority as a spokesman for the party line of the period, and Ella's middle-class perceptions, such as her lament for the death of the English countryside, are enriched and complicated rather than simply discredited by exposure to his orthodox Marxism.

Ella's bourgeois Englishness enables her to discover the effects of sexual inequality without automatically assigning them to subsidiary status within an overarching system of interpretations. The problem to which she is passionately committed has, as Friedan observed, "no name"; because she cannot "name" it, Ella is able to perceive it as important. She and Paul come to refer to the letters constituting her "weekly dose of misery" as "Mrs Brown," a provisional and synecdochic tag that "names" by laying stress on the personal rather than by locating the phenomenon within a theoretical schema.[29] The same kind of stress characterizes Anna's controversial defense through Ella of the vaginal orgasm as "emotion and nothing else, felt as emotion and expressed in sensations that are indistinguishable from emotion" (p. 215). Ella insists on fidelity to what she feels, in the face of "evidence" maintaining that her feelings are irrelevant or, worse, that there are experts better qualified than she to know her responses. Paul's anecdote about the female doctors' boycott of a hospital lecture on the superiority of the clitoral orgasm reinforces the implication that when expertise is invoked against experience the expertise will be male, the experience female. "My dear Ella, don't you know what the great revolution of our time is?" Paul asks. "The Russian revolution, the Chinese revolution—they're nothing at all. The real revolution is, women against men" (p. 213). Ella demurs, but this version of the "revolution" permeates the Yellow notebook, pulling her story away from its ostensible focus on "the third," the stereotypical feminine ideal projected as an emblem of

---

[29]Virginia Woolf uses "Mrs Brown" in a startlingly similar way—to counter Arnold Bennett's and the Edwardian realists' tendency to subsume the personal to a mass of economic and social documentation. See Woolf, "Mr Bennett and Mrs Brown," in *The Captain's Death Bed and Other Essays* (London: Hogarth Press, 1950), pp. 99–111. Woolf's writings and her writing practices may have had more influence on Lessing than scholars have yet been able to document; for instance, the "degeneration" of the notebooks into collections of newspaper clippings is suggestively reminiscent of the notebooks of clippings that Woolf assembled during the years in which she was preparing to write *Three Guineas*.

sanity, and recentering it around the behavior of men in a society where women's subsidiary and instrumental status is taken for granted.

The use of this theme in the Yellow notebook is so arresting that it conditioned the early reception of the whole novel; as Lessing later noted with irritation, "I learned that I had written a tract about the sex war, and fast discovered that nothing I said then could change that diagnosis."[30] Her treatment of the "sex war" theme is especially volatile because she has chosen to tell—and retell over and over—one of the most familiar stories of the postwar period: the tragedy of the organization man, hemmed in and thwarted by convention and enforced domesticity, broken on the rack of postindustrial anti-individualism or in active rebellion against pressures to conform.[31] She always tells it, however, from the point of view of a female figure whose customary function is to symbolize either

---

[30]Lessing, 1972 introduction to *The Golden Notebook*, p. x.

[31]Sloan Wilson's *Man in the Gray Flannel Suit* is a paradigm of this story, but in a 1962 essay Ihab Hassan argued that virtually all important contemporary novels reacted against "the normative image of our culture," which "can be projected in a series of preposterous or unctuous cliches. It is the image of an organization man who foregoes the ulcerous rewards of an executive suite, pottering about a house with a cracked picture window looking into the crack of another picture window, and viewing with apathy the coming caesars of our imperial state, the hidden persuaders and clowns of commerce of Madison Avenue." According to Hassan, writers reacting to this "normative image" range from J. D. Salinger to Saul Bellow to Jack Kerouac, all having in common "the figure of the rebel-victim [who] incarnates the eternal dialectic between the primary Yes and everlasting No" and who is "perhaps one of the last exemplars of a vanishing conception of man"—"man" being both a universal and a masculine denomination, as his subsequent discussion makes clear ("The Character of Post-war Fiction in America," in *On Contemporary Literature*, ed. Kostelanetz, pp. 38, 40). One writer that Hassan does not mention (he was far too minor, even at the time, to figure in such an essay) is Clancy Sigal, with whom Lessing had an affair and who is the prototype of Saul Green. Sigal's novel *Going Away* (London: Jonathan Cape, 1963), is an *On the Road*–style *mensch* novel, almost compulsive in its elaboration of clearly autobiographical minutiae. At times its bravura overwriting suggests the "romantic tough school of writing" that Lessing parodies on pp. 539–41. More often, passages recall excerpts from the diaries of Saul Green recorded in the Blue notebook. For example, reflecting on the information that a woman he had slept with had been picked up later the same night walking naked through the streets of Los Angeles, Sigal's narrator muses, "Why was I feeling so horrified, so utterly paralysed by shame? Hers hadn't been the only hand I had held right up to the gates of Norwalk" (p. 13). Saul Green foregoes the nod to horror and paralysis: "Got a letter from Jake in Detroit. Mavis cut her wrists with a razor. They got her to hospital in time. Pity, a nice girl" (p. 572).

freedom or thralldom (or, in a familiar irony peculiar to the genre, both), a figure who does not customarily *have* a point of view beyond the possible adjunct role implied in articulating the hero's problem.[32] In effect, she tells the other side of the dominant story of the fifties, and the act of telling the other side alters the story irrevocably. In the Yellow notebook the saga of the misplaced organization man who tries to alleviate the pain and ennui of midcentury alienation with an extramarital affair is told, first at length, in the section dealing with Ella's five-year relationship with Paul Tanner, then more briefly in the episode involving Cy Maitland, then very briefly and explosively in the story of the unnamed Canadian. In effect Ella suffers through shorter and progressively more emphatic synopses of an encounter in which the salient features are unequal power, manipulation, and complete inability of the dominant partner to understand the inferior partner, or even to understand that anyone is there to understand.

The effect of these reiterations is shattering. It is not, however, Ella who shatters, succumbing to the psychic self-division Anna had planned for her, but the narrative itself that "breaks down" into different short fictions, at first naturalized as Ella's projections (she "looks inward" to find them) but soon supplanting *The Shadow of the Third* entirely. The fourth Yellow notebook section consists entirely of short pieces of writing, numbered and captioned "A SHORT STORY" or "A SHORT NOVEL" and culminating in a parody entitled "THE ROMANTIC TOUGH SCHOOL OF WRITING" that accurately captures the sentimentality and banality intrinsic to the saga of the alienated rebel as young artist, this time the American "political" version:

> Dave scratched his crotch, slow, owl-scratching pure Dave. "Jeez, Mike," he said, "you'll write it someday, for us all." He stammered, inarticulate, not-winged-with-words. "You'll write it, hey feller? And how our souls were ruined here on the snow-white Manhattan pavement, the capitalist-money-mammon hound-of-hell hot on our heels?" "Gee, Dave, I love you," I said then, my boy's soul twisted with love. I hit him then, square to the jaw-bone, stammering with love-for-the-

---

[32]As Anna does in the diatribe beginning, "Like all Americans you've got mother-trouble" (p. 581). Significantly, this is the passage in which Anna identifies her own "banal over-simplification." She also accuses Saul of "feeling pleasure because you've provoked me into screaming at you"—she is, after all, also screaming *about* him.

world, love-for-my-friends, for the Daves and the Mikes and the Bud-
dies. [p. 541]

This passage is followed by a single sentence, "If I've gone back
to pastiche, then it's time to stop," and on that note the Yellow
notebook ends forever, ostensibly "blocked" by Anna's hypercritical
awareness of the conventions conditioning her fragmented culture.
Yet it is impossible to take at face value the thesis that such parody
is simply a debased kind of writing, evidence of a divided consciousness fated to exhaust itself in sterile and meaningless productions. Anna's construction of her "writer's block" as a decline
from wholeness and of self-conscious art forms as a degeneration
from a healthily unreflective realism is as sentimental and banal as
the assumptions of the "tough guy school" she parodies, implying
a similarly romantic nostalgia for lost innocence. Furthermore, the
parody and the sketches constituting the final section of the Yellow
notebook do not function as dead ends within the novel as a whole.
On the contrary, they serve as multiple openings into the accounts
of psychic "breakdown" that follow in the Blue and Golden notebooks and in the concluding chapter of "Free Women," foreshad-
owing selected events and thus glossing different aspects of these
accounts while emphasizing the variant cultural codes at work in
each. In effect, they add more voices, more versions, to the voices
and versions already licensed by the convention of the frame story
and the imbedded notebooks. And in the process they reinforce a
growing awareness that in *The Golden Notebook* "the truth" is not a
fixed reality that lurks behind the distortions of narrative form but
a product of tellings and retellings. Or rather, that there is no truth
apart from the telling, no real story, no authorized version, no vantage point that allows experience to be viewed as a whole.

IV

Although in many respects Ella is a character as developed and
individualized as Anna herself, her story stays shakily imbedded in
Anna's. Hints that the relation of container to contained might be
reversed, so that Ella might emerge as author of Anna's story ("A
man and a woman—yes"), can be reconciled to the governing prem-

ise of "real" and "fictional" levels, albeit laboriously: such fore-shadowings were "actually" written by Anna at a later date and deal with her own "real" experiences, which she fictionalizes through the device of Ella-as-writer.[33] According to this naturalization Anna goes to such lengths because her "writer's block" has forced her to compartmentalize different aspects of her life as different kinds of discourse. Psychological fragmentation thus becomes the convention that allows the text to remain coherent.

But the requirement of depicting psychological fragmentation seems to elicit descriptive techniques that are also "cracked" or "split,": essentially negative in content, sketchy, tentative, presented as evidence of failure. That the experience of "breakdown" eludes description seems to be one of the most important things that can be said about it, and over and over Lessing manipulates a vocabulary of negative words and phrases to reiterate that the central truth of this kind of event remains out of reach and unarticulated. The third-person narrator of "Free Women" reports that Anna encountered "a reality different from anything she had known before as reality," but can describe it only in terms of what it was not: "It was not being 'depressed'; or being 'unhappy'; or feeling 'discouraged'; the essence of the experience was that such words, like joy or happiness, were meaningless" (p. 652). Similarly, Anna writes in the Blue notebook, "I *knew*, but of course the word, written, cannot convey the quality of this knowing" (p. 589), and in a key passage from the Golden notebook generalizes these observations further, codifying a theory that makes "language" a mute gesture toward the ineffable: "The fact is, the real experience can't be described. I think, bitterly, that a row of asterisks, like an old-fashioned novel, might be better. Or a symbol of some kind, a circle perhaps, or a square. Anything at all, but not words. The people who have been there, in the place in themselves where words, patterns, order, dissolve, will know what I mean and the others won't" (pp. 633–34). Such passages employ a narrative strategy that is a virtual *via negativa*. On the most obvious level, "the people who have been

---

[33]Passages in the Blue notebook reinforce such a naturalization. For example, Anna writes, "I came across an entry which frightened me, because I had already written it, out of some other kind of knowledge, in my yellow notebook" (p. 572).

there, in the place in themselves where words, pattern, order, dissolve," are the only possible audience for Anna's comments; they are defined as the only people who could have any idea what she means. Yet insofar as these statements describe the incapacity of "language" to mean, they are meaningful statements, and insofar as they are meaningful statements they foreground the materiality of the novel, the fact that it is a construct of language. In such passages the fictional discourse is turned back on itself, calling attention to the conventions according to which novels signify, while framing and pointing up the implication that something significant is *not* being said. "Cracks" and "gaps" thus function as elements of description, implying the existence of something utterly new and unrepresentable, at least within the realist tradition.

Furthermore, Lessing does not confine "breakdown" to the realm of characterization. The climactic section of *The Golden Notebook* in which Anna's psychological "breakdown" occurs is itself broken down into two irreconcilable versions: the long, intense first-person account in the Blue and Golden notebooks describing the interaction between Anna and Saul Green, and the shorter, more dispassionate third-person account in "Free Women" describing Anna's descent into obsession and her deliverance by an American identified only as Milt. Taken separately, neither of these narratives exceeds the defining conditions of realism. The diary form of the first imposes a rigorously chronological order of discourse on events that paradoxically include loss of a sense of time (pp. 593–94); it also motivates a preoccupation with documenting exactly when in the course of the narrated action each entry was written. The deliberately traditional form of the second—Lessing has spoken of "Free Women" as "an absolutely whole conventional novel"[34]—presents Anna's collapse as the inevitable consequence of Anna's absorption in the chaos of current affairs and avoids replicating the conclusion of Ella's novel about suicide only by bringing in a fortuitous rescuer, another horrific version of the "real man," who confesses ingenuously after he has restored Anna to sanity, "I can't sleep with women I like" (p. 660). But at this point in *The Golden Notebook*, realist conventions

---

[34]Florence Howe, "A Conversation," p. 11.

no longer suffice to create a framework within which these two stories can coexist. Both have as their protagonist a woman named Anna who is a "blocked" novelist and is going through some sort of crisis in the company of an American man: both are clearly versions of a single story and not, for instance, chronicles of two different "breakdowns" suffered in sequence by the same character. Indeed, the emphasis and tone, not to mention the conclusions, of the two accounts are so different that the Annas in each cannot be the same character. "Anna" has undergone a textual split, and in the course of *The Golden Notebook* she is never put back together again.

In the account set out in the Blue and Golden notebooks "breakdown" is an educational process, a "breaking through,"[35] which Anna undertakes by deciding to enter into Saul Green's "madness." The experience at first forces to extremes her habitual self-division into active participant and detached, critical observer. "Meanwhile my anxiety state is permanent, I've forgotten what it is like to wake up normally," she reports; "yet I watch this state I'm in, and even think: Well, I'll never suffer from my own anxiety state, so I might just as well experience someone else's while I get the chance" (p. 575). But the aim of the educational process is to dissolve boundaries, to the point where Anna longs to "be free of [her] own ordering, commenting memory" and feels her "sense of identity fade" (p. 585). As she moves further into "madness," division becomes proliferation, prompted by a need to learn that provokes her to ask Saul at one point, "What do you think this thing is that makes people like us have to experience everything? We're driven by something to be as many different things or people as possible" (p. 613). The question affirms a hitherto unrecognized positive aspect in the myriad examples of personal fragmentation that build up to this climax: role playing, discrepancies between spoken and body language, cliched speeches made up of disparate shards of cultural discourses. To *be* something or someone different appears in this passage to be the most intense and authentic kind of knowing. By a peculiar in-

---

[35]Roberta Rubenstein plays on the dual implications of "break" in these two formulations throughout *The Novelistic Vision of Doris Lessing*.

version, fragmentation has become comprehension. The rhetoric of denial accordingly grows more intrusive, while long, cumulative sentences incorporate perceptions linked for the first time:

> There was a kind of shifting of the balances of my brain, of the way I had been thinking, the same kind of realignment as when, a few days before, words like democracy, liberty, freedom, had faded under pressure of a new sort of understanding of the real movement of the world towards dark, hardening power. I *knew*, but of course the word, written, cannot convey the quality of this knowing, that whatever already is has its logic and its force, that the great armouries of the world have their inner force, and that my terror, the real nerve-terror of the nightmare, was part of the force. I felt this, like a vision, in a new kind of knowing. And I knew that the cruelty and the spite and the I, I, I, I of Saul and of Anna were part of the logic of war; and I knew how strong these emotions were, in a way that would never leave me, would become part of how I saw the world. [pp. 588–89]

By contrast, Anna's "breakdown" in the "Free Women" account is presented as a direct reflection of her fragmented culture, rendered graphically in the image of a room whose four walls are completely covered with newspaper clippings. In this context, to break down is merely to succumb to a sort of societal entropy, for "madness" leads to nothing more than further disintegration. Milt accordingly intervenes as savior rather than playing the less familiar role of companion schizophrenic that is assigned to Saul Green.[36] The narrator remains cool and detached and, like the narrator of "To Room Nineteen," sets up the situation at the outset in a way that implicitly closes off possibility: "Anna discovered she was spending most of her time doing nothing at all; and decided the remedy for her condition was a man. She prescribed this for herself like a medicine" (p. 648). And Anna and Milt speak almost exclusively in cliches, which they recognize and acknowledge but seem unable to go beyond:

> "They said you were a left-winger," said Anna in appeal; interested that this was what she instinctively said in explanation of the state of affairs.

[36]Both Lessing and Clancy Sigal participated in R. D. Laing's early experiments with hallucinogenically induced "schizophrenic" states, and many of Lessing's insights in the "breakdown" scene reflect Laing's.

"Vintage, post-war."
"I'm waiting for you to say: I and the other three socialists in the States are going to . . . "
"The other *four*." [p. 655]

Like the heightened rhetoric of the preceding account, such ironic exchanges are responses to the problem of "language" that has been a preoccupation of the novel. But rather than trying to articulate the radically new, the characters in "Free Women" are merely self-conscious about their manipulation of commonplaces. Irony distances them from the vocabulary of an exhausted tradition without making them any less dependent on that tradition. Milt's leave-taking is almost painfully reminiscent of Richard—"No, but let's preserve the forms, the *forms* at least of . . . " (p. 664)— and conventional form triumphs in "Free Women," leading the discourse inexorably toward closure on a note that amounts to a categorical betrayal of the promise held out at the beginning. In the course of the scene in Molly's flat that opens both "Free Women" and the novel itself, the narrator reports,

> That they were both "insecure" and "unrooted," words which dated from the era of Mother Sugar, they both freely acknowledged. But Anna had recently been learning to use these words in a different way, not as something to be apologised for, but as flags or banners for an attitude that amounted to a different philosophy. She had enjoyed fantasies of saying to Molly: We've had the wrong attitude to the whole thing, and it's Mother Sugar's fault—what is this security and balance that's supposed to be so good? What's wrong with living emotionally from hand-to-mouth in a world that's changing as fast as it is? [p. 10]

But by the concluding section of "Free Women," which is also the last section of *The Golden Notebook*, both Anna and Molly have opted for security and roots, although their calculated use of irony signals that they are aware of the extent of the compromise. Anna plans to do social work and involve herself with the Labour party; Molly has committed herself to a loveless marriage. "So we're both going to be integrated with British life at its roots," says Molly, and Anna replies, "I was carefully avoiding that tone" (p. 666). But the tone is necessary if accommodation is to be distinguished from despair. The catchphrase that at the opening of the story signifies the intimacy between the two women, "Odd, isn't it?" (p. 3), recurs at the end, on the occasion of their separation: "It's all very odd, isn't it Anna?" (p. 666)."Oddness" has become the pervasive quality of a world distanced by irony, and having no more to discuss about such a world, the two women kiss and separate.

But "Free Women" is not the only narrative in *The Golden Notebook*, and the conclusion of "Free Women" is not the only basis for coming to a conclusion about the import of the novel as a whole. Speculating on the probable success of her convenient marriage, Molly observes, "There's nothing like knowing the exact dimensions of the bed you're going to fit yourself into" (p. 666), and the remark resonates as an epitaph for the story that Lessing herself ironically proffers as truncated and crushed into a predetermined shape by the requirements of a Procrustean realist tradition. The notebooks, on the other hand, present a very different resolution to the story about a novelist named Anna, one that directly addresses her "writer's block" and in the process "cracks" and "splits" the containing form, completely unsettling the levels of "fictional" and "real" narration. The Golden notebook also ends with a separation, but that Anna and Saul part is less important than the each supplies the other with a new beginning, the opening line of a novel to be written. Anna's gift to Saul, the sentence "On a dry hillside in Algeria, a soldier watched the moonlight glinting on his rifle" (p. 642), becomes the beginning of a short novel that "was later published and did rather well," according to one of the two bracketed notes appended to the close of this section (p. 643).[37] Saul's gift to Anna, however, is the sentence "The two women were alone in the London flat" (p. 639), and this sentence is Lessing's own opening to "Free Women" and thus to *The Golden Notebook*. The gesture might be interpreted as indicating

[37]The brackets recall Tommy's remark in "Free Women," "Why do . . . you bracket bits off? You give importance to one kind of feeling and not to others? How do you decide what's important and what isn't?" (p. 272). Certainly they seem intended to separate "editorial" or "narratorial" passages from those written by Anna, but within the naturalization such separations are especially dubious. At this point the whole framework of *The Golden Notebook* seems designed to force the questions: who is the author of the synopsis of Saul's novel? Who is explaining that it "did rather well"? When naturalization runs rampant, the conventions of naturalization themselves "break down": become exposed as flimsy and arbitrary devices for imposing hierarchical order on a narrative that gains little from the imposition.

merely that Anna is the author of "Free Women" and that "Free Women" is "really" framed by the notebooks rather than the other way around, in which case "Free Women" becomes simply another "fictionalization" of the "real" Anna's experiences, and the other characters in it emerge as further inventions or projections. Following this line of reasoning, Roberta Rubenstein points out that the Tommy of this section might well be a personification of Anna's "inner critic."[38] But "Free Women" is not distinct from other sections of the novel, and in pursuing the logic of naturalization to its implicitly paradoxical conclusion Rubenstein brings criticism up against the limits of naturalization as a strategy for reading *The Golden Notebook*. She points out that the "editorial" comments linking "Free Women" to the notebooks cannot be attributed to an omniscient narrator once the omniscient narrator of "Free Women" has been revealed to be Anna; given the continuity of the narration, if Anna wrote "Free Women" she also wrote *The Golden Notebook*. Furthermore, the elusiveness of "the truth" has been one of Anna's central preoccupations, to the point where Anna has "already conceded that even in the Blue notebook/diary she fictionalizes her experiences," and as a consequence it is impossible to discern which aspects, if any, of the notebooks are not "fictional." Anna's practice of using writing as a means of "splitting" or "projecting" herself into different characters thus has no intrinsic boundaries: once the precedent is established, there is no compelling reason for maintaining that *any* of the characters described has an independent existence. And so Rubenstein proposes that even Saul Green is finally "real" only "within the layer of mimetic reality invented by Anna in the Blue and Golden notebooks," for "he becomes part of her own invention as soon as one moves back from that frame."[39] He is "really," that is, only another aspect of Anna's fragmented consciousness, and the climactic Golden notebook section of the novel is therefore a drama of self-projection, not a communion of two psyches.

Ultimately this argument would seem to lead to the conclusion that all parts of the novel are equally "fictional," a conclusion making

[38]Rubenstein, *The Novelistic Vision*, p. 103.
[39]Ibid., pp. 104–5.

the "real"/"fictional" opposition irrelevant and indicating that the relation of one account to the other cannot be one of container to contained. But Rubenstein requires a controlling consciousness to preside over *The Golden Notebook* as its principle of unity and argues that "the narrative must establish a trust for the reader" by providing "a consistent mimetic reality supporting . . . the major characters of the novel." She consequently posits an "invisible Anna" who is "in fact the 'editor' of the entire work, interposed between the fragmented Anna of the notebooks and fictions and Doris Lessing herself."[40] This "Anna" is neither the character in "Free Women" who is the author of the notebooks nor the character in the notebooks who is the author of "Free Women." Like "the Third" of the Yellow notebook, this third "Anna" is a sort of Jungian shadow, representing the "real" precisely inasmuch as she is *not* present within the fictional frame of reference, for she is not a character at all.

But if the authorial "Anna" is not in the story, she is completely unknowable. There is no basis for calling her "Anna" or for supposing that the experiences she recounts are in any sense her own. At this point in the naturalization "Anna" becomes indistinguishable from Lessing, and the fictional "real" becomes indistinguishable from reality.

Rubenstein's argument suggests that the attempt to resolve the two accounts by invoking a hierarchy of ontological levels first necessitates a drastic kind of hermeneutics, which insists on a "real" meaning violently at odds with the apparent one, and finally reduces the "real"/"fictional" opposition to meaninglessness anyway.[41] What seems to be important about the accounts is not that one contains the other but that each is a version of the story about social

[40]Ibid., pp. 102, 107.

[41]The distinction between levels of reality—between fact and fiction within the narrative—is blurred in other ways. In the dream-vision of the Golden notebook Anna relates that she was required "to go back and look at scenes from my life," but one of these scenes is from the "fictional" Yellow notebook and involves the "character" Paul Tanner, who is "merged" with the "real" Michael, who had appeared to be Paul's prototype (pp. 616–17). And Saul, instructing Anna on how to begin her novel, says, "I'm going to give you the first sentence then. There are *the two women you are, Anna*. Write down: The two women were alone in the London flat" (p. 639, my emphasis), a statement insinuating that even Molly, prominent in "Free Women" and the Blue notebook and "fictionalized" as Julia in the Yellow notebook, is an invention and projection of Anna.

and personal "breakdown." Neither version is definitive. If the conclusion of "Free Women" emphasizes compromise and debilitating
irony as effects of the closure imposed by traditional realism, the
self-reflexive "conclusion" of the Golden notebook resolves anxiety
into art, in effect subsuming the fragmentation of the social order
to the novelist's unifying vision and affirming that the way to redeem
the time is to write about it. Lessing thus contrasts a realist and an
implicitly modernist resolution, the first subordinating "art" to "life"
(rather than being cured of her "writer's block" Anna moves on to
more pressing concerns) and the second subordinating "life" to "art"
(the "writer's block" becomes the sole obstacle that must be "broken
through," and production of *The Golden Notebook* itself is evidence
of a return to wholeness). If the realist ending is insufficient, the
Mobius-strip modernist "ending" is adequate only if artistic creation
is the *summum bonum*, that is, if the "true artist" is placed outside
and above social reality, like Stephen Daedelus's god of creation,
"within or above or behind [her] handiwork, invisible, refined out
of existence," or in Mrs Marks's more homespun formulation, creating out of an inability to live. Of course, this view of the artist has
been thoroughly discredited within the novel.

The two narratives are thus not only irreconcilable; neither can be
construed as taking precedence over the other. *The Golden Notebook*
has no single "real" ending, nor is one ending offered as preferable.
On the contrary, the two narratives, both alone and in combination,
emerge as profoundly unsatisfactory. Lessing has "named" the
problem as disintegration, fragmentation, incoherence, but she has
not resolved it, either thematically or formally. Rather, she has suggested that resolution may not be precisely what is called for, that
"gaps" and "splits" in the text, as in the personality, suggest ways
of being more than one thing or person, and that this tentative
realizing of multiple possibilities more effectively suggests the extent
of the hitherto unknown or unrepresented than any structure imposing coherence.

Such an analysis suggests that by the time she wrote *The Golden
Notebook*, Lessing had ceased to view novelistic coherence in terms
of "a climate of ethical judgement" and saw in its claims of wholeness evidence of a limitation more damaging in that it was not
perceived. To adopt Philippe Sollers's description, both the realist

and the modernist novel had become for her "the way this society speaks to itself" and thus an instrument of repression, "the manifestation of power in our time and a key to its mechanical, closed everyday unconsciousness."[42] To resist this "mechanical, closed everyday unconsciousness" she systematically subverted the most familiar forms that the novel has taken, subverting as well the assumption that such forms are the natural structure of all possible experience. Within the notebook accounts, for instance, "the game" that Anna plays is one analogue of novelistic form that parodies conventional notions of coherence. Something like a meditative exercise, "the game" initially seems to be a means of expanding consciousness and overcoming illusory divisions. To play it, Anna begins by "creating" in her imagination her immediate surroundings, then slowly enlarges her scope to "create" the house, the street, and, taking an aerial perspective, the city, the country, the continent, and the world—all the time keeping clearly in mind the early stages so as to achieve "a simultaneous knowledge of vastness and of smallness" (p. 548). But the kind of "simultaneous knowledge" that she seeks—in effect the omniscience of the nineteenth-century narrator combined with the omnipotence of the refined-out-of-existence twentieth-century artist—presumes a position of externality for the "creator" that is a kind of control: significantly, Anna envisions herself as placed *above* the spinning world that her mind encompasses. "Knowledge" of this sort presumes that there is a position of observation, and thus an angle of vision, that is "correct" and in this way imposes a particular form: the thing known is contained, distanced, and fixed. Anna's published novel, *Frontiers of War*, was a product of this presumption and resulted from Anna's having made a set of events from her past into a "story," a product of hindsight, a re-viewing of experience *sub specie resolutionis*. She subsequently identifies her attitude toward these events as "lying nostalgia" (p. 63), and the "lie" is the one imposed by the requirements of "a story" as she has perceived it, a yearning for the apparent stasis and finish of a closed-off past comprehended completely.

It is only at the climax of her "breakdown" in the Golden notebook, when Anna finds herself viewing "conventionally well-made

[42]Sollers, "The Novel and the Experience of Limits," p. 61.

films" that parody the conventions she herself has taken for granted in imaging this part of her life, that she realizes how limited her vision has been. "And what makes you think the emphasis you have put on it is the correct emphasis?" inquires the projectionist, who in this dream-vision embodies the ambiguous connotations of "project" while playing ironic Virgil to her Dante; and she notes the parodically Marxist use of the word *correct*, finally throwing into question the notion of a coherent world view arising from a privileged viewpoint (p. 619). "Literature is analysis after the event," she had written earlier (p. 228), and much of the experience she undergoes has underscored that literature, as she has always understood it, invariably falsifies by refusing to acknowledge that "after the event" is only one perspective. But now the projectionist pushes further. "How would June Boothby see that time? I bet you can't do June Boothby," he says (p. 620), suddenly foregrounding someone who in Anna's memory—and in *The Golden Notebook*—functions as a minor character. The irresistible implication is that every perspective is as "correct" as every other perspective, that the whole is constituted by all possible perspectives, and that therefore an apprehension of the whole is, strictly speaking, impossible. If fragmented perception is dangerous, the serious danger lies in mistaking a fragment for the truth in its entirety.

Because there is ultimately no one "correct" perspective, *The Golden Notebook* refuses to resolve into a single "real" story. The two accounts in "Free Women" and the notebooks place different emphases on the discussion of the writer's role in a disintegrating society without arriving at the last word—without exhausting the possibilities for further stories. In *The Golden Notebook* Lessing is concerned to create the conditions that allow the future to make an appearance, not to indicate what shape it might take. Many of her later books, however, from *The Four-Gated City* to the *Canopus in Argos* series, deal very literally with "the future," with action taking place in a time well after the time of writing, exploring prophetic genres from apocalyptic to space fiction and ultimately taking their direction from the insistence of the Blue and Golden notebooks that visionary experience cannot be entirely absorbed into psychological or political explanatory systems. Others, including *The Summer before the Dark* and the two pseudonymous Jane Somers novels, have protagonists who resemble Ella in playing traditional female roles in preponderantly female worlds and might be the ironic products of Ella's musing, for unwillingly and often unwittingly they "break their own form, as it were."[43] In aiming "to shape a book which would make its own comment, a wordless statement: to talk through the way it was shaped,"[44] Lessing dispersed both character and plot, challenging the claims of a single holistic vision to contain the truth. In the process she at once fulfilled Anna's demand for "a book powered with an intellectual or moral passion strong enough to create order, to create a new way of looking at life" (p. 61) and opened up "cracks" and "gaps" into which future productions might pour, in diverse and unpredictable shapes.

[43]The brilliant 1985 novel *The Good Terrorist* suggests a return to realism with a different, far more cynical ideology behind it: "postrealism" is one of the terms that might apply to it.

[44]Lessing, 1972 Preface to *The Golden Notebook*, p. xiv.

Chapter 3

Romance, Marginality, Matrilineage: *The Color Purple*

The publication of *The Color Purple* transformed Alice Walker from an indubitably serious black writer whose fiction belonged to a tradition of gritty, if occasionally "magical," realism into a popular novelist, with all the perquisites and drawbacks attendant on that position. Unlike either *The Third Life of Grange Copeland* (1970) or *Meridian* (1976), *The Color Purple* gained immediate and widespread public acceptance, winning both the Pulitzer Prize and the American Book Award for 1982–1983. At the same time, however, it generated immediate and widespread critical unease over what appeared to be manifest flaws in its composition. Robert Towers, writing in the *New York Review of Books*, concluded on the evidence of *The Color Purple* that "Alice Walker still has a lot to learn about plotting and structuring what is clearly intended to be a realistic novel." His opinion was shared by many reviewers, who pointed out variously that in the last third of the book the narrator-protagonist Celie and her friends are propelled toward a fairy-tale happy ending with more velocity than credibility; that the letters from Nettie, with their disconcertingly literate depictions of life in an African village, intrude into the middle of the main action with little apparent motivation or warrant; and that the device of the letters to God is especially unrealistic inasmuch as it foregoes the concretizing details that have traditionally given the epistolary form its peculiar verisimilitude: the secret writing

place, the cache, the ruses to enable posting letters, and especially the letters received in return.[1]

Indeed, the violations of realist convention are so flagrant that
they might well call into question whether *The Color Purple* "is clearly
intended to be a realistic novel," especially as there are indications
that at least some of those aspects of the novel discounted by reviewers as flaws may constitute its links to modes of writing other
than Anglo-American nineteenth-century realism. For example,
Henry Louis Gates, Jr., has recently located the letters to God within
an Afro-American tradition deriving from slave narrative, a tradition
in which the act of writing is linked to a powerful deity who "speaks"
through scripture and bestows literacy as an act of grace.[2] For Gates,
concern with finding a voice, which he sees as the defining feature
of Afro-American literature, becomes the context for the allusive
affinities between Celie's letters and the "free indirect 'narrative of
division' " that characterizes the acknowledged predecessor of *The
Color Purple*, Zora Neale Hurston's 1937 novel *Their Eyes Were Watching God*.[3]

Gates's paradigm suggests how misleading it may be to assume

[1]Robert Towers, *New York Review of Books*, 12 August 1982, 36. Adam Gussow notes
the "sudden swerve" into Nettie's letters and calls it "one of the novel's few weak-
nesses" (*Chicago Review* 34, no. 1 [1983], 125). Maria K. Mootry-Ikerionwu opposes
Walker's ideas to her "craft," "which doesn't quite carry off her vision," and finds
the letters to God as improbable as Celie's passivity (*"The Color Purple*: A Moral Tale,"
CLA Journal 27, no. 3 [1984], 347). Tamar Katz elegantly points out how *The Color
Purple* refrains from exploiting many of the most characteristic conventions of the
epistolary form in " 'Show me how to do like you': Didacticism and Epistolary Form
in Alice Walker's *The Color Purple*" (Unpublished paper, Cornell University), p. 8.
Significantly, it is a Renaissance scholar, Ruth El Saffar, who suggests the genre with
which I believe the novel is most closely allied; in a review of *The Color Purple* in the
International Fiction Review 12, no. 1 (1985), she writes, "the discovery of 'Pa's' usur-
pation affects the novel itself, turning it from history, with all its emphasis on power
and control, to romance, whose main focus is love and redemption" (p. 15).

[2]These motifs are summed up succinctly in a quotation of Rebecca Cox Jackson
that serves as a headnote to Gates's Walker chapter, "I am only a pen in His hand."
Henry Louis Gates, Jr., "Color Me Zora: Alice Walker's (Re)writing of the Speakerly
Text," in his *The Signifying Monkey: A Theory of Afro-American Literary Criticism* (New
York: Oxford University Press, 1988), p. 239.

[3]Gates maintains that the letters to God thus represent a further turn on Hurston's
own invention of a discourse accommodating both "dialect" and standard English:
"Celie's written voice to God, her reader, tropes the written yet never uttered voice
of free indirect discourse which is the predominant vehicle of narrative commentary
in Hurston's novel" (p. 243).

that mainstream realist criteria are appropriate for evaluating *The Color Purple*. But the Afro-American preoccupation with voice as a primary element unifying both the speaking subject and the text as a whole does not deal with many of the more disquieting structural features of Walker's novel. For instance, while the letters from Nettie clearly illustrate Nettie's parallel acquisition of her own voice, a process that enables her to arrive at conclusions very like Celie's under very different circumstances, the Afro-American tradition sheds little light on the central *place* these letters occupy in the narrative or on why the plot takes this sudden jump into geographically and culturally removed surroundings. And Gates's subtle explication of the ramifications of "voice" once Walker has reconstrued the term to designate a *written* discourse does not address the problematic ending, in which the disparate members of Celie's extended family come together as if drawn by a cosmic magnet—and as if in defiance of the most minimal demands of narrative probability.

The example of *Their Eyes Were Watching God* tends to compound these problems rather than provide a precedent that helps explain them, for Hurston's most famous novel has also been judged flawed, and for many of the same reasons. To a certain extent, placing *Their Eyes* in the context of an Afro-American tradition that Hurston herself did much to document reveals how central the act of storytelling is in this book, to the point where Janie's discovery and use of her narrating voice emerges as the major action.[4] This context helps explain the tendency of the story *about* storytelling to usurp the ostensible main plot of Janie's quest for happiness with a man—for example, the apparently disproportionate emphasis given to the

[4]Hurston trained as an anthropologist at Barnard with Franz Boas. Her book-length study of black folklore, *Mules and Men* (1935; Bloomington: Indiana University Press, 1978), serves as a useful thematic and rhetorical source for *Their Eyes Were Watching God*. See especially Barbara Johnson, "Thresholds of Difference: Structures of Address in Zora Neale Hurston," *Critical Inquiry* 12 (Autumn 1985), 278–89. In "Reading Zora: Discourse and Rhetoric in *Their Eyes Were Watching God*" (Unpublished manuscript, Yale University), Henry Louis Gates, Jr., and Barbara Johnson maintain, "The very subject of this text would seem to be not primarily Janie's quest, but the emulation of the phonetic, grammatical, and lexical structures of actual speech" (p. 33). Elizabeth Meese places a more overtly feminist construction on the role of voice in "Orality and Textuality in Zora Neale Hurston's *Their Eyes Were Watching God*," in her *Crossing the Double-Cross: The Practice of Feminist Criticism* (Chapel Hill: University of North Carolina Press, 1986), pp. 41–53.

digressive "co-talkin' " of such minor characters as Hicks and Coker in Eatonville or to the rhetoric of the "skin games" played by Ed Dockery, Bootyny, and Sop-de-Bottom on the muck and the exuberant fabulation that takes over chapter 6 so completely that the story of the mule "freed" at Janie's instigation turns completely away from realism and becomes a beast fable, with buzzards as parson and congregation chanting a parodic litany over the carrion.[5]

But once again the Afro-American paradigm leaves untouched some of the most problematic structural elements of this novel, elements that according to many critics constitute lapses or flaws in its composition. Dianne Sadoff makes the case most persuasively, and most sympathetically inasmuch as she discerns "marks, fissures, and traces of 'inferiorization' " that amount to "scars of disguise or concealment because [Hurston] is black and female—doubly alienated from a white and patriarchal mainstream literature."[6] Sadoff views *Their Eyes Were Watching God* as a celebration of heterosexual love that is undercut by Hurston's own ambivalence over the compatibility of marriage and the creative "voice" that produces fiction. The ambivalence is figured most acutely in the misogynistic attitudes and behavior that Hurston tacitly ascribes to Janie's third husband and great love, Tea Cake, and in the action of the scene where, according to the covert logic of the narrative, if not the overt logic of explication, Janie murders Tea Cake, just as she has murdered her previous husband, Jody Starks. As Sadoff observes, "Hurston has motivated her narrative, perhaps unconsciously, to act out her rage against male domination and to free Janie, a figure for herself, from all men."[7]

In making the "marks" and "scars" that she perceives in Hurston's novel the inevitable consequence of Hurston's doubly marginalized social position, Sadoff employs a version of the Gilbert and Gubar "anxiety of authorship" model pioneered in *The Madwoman in the Attic.*[8] In the process, however, she underscores problems with this

---

[5]Zora Neale Hurston, *Their Eyes Were Watching God* (Urbana: University of Illinois Press, 1978), pp. 58–59; 200–2, 81–97, hereafter cited parenthetically in the text.
[6]Dianne F. Sadoff, "Black Matrilineage: The Case of Alice Walker and Zora Neale Hurston," *Signs: A Journal of Women in Culture and Society* 11, no. 1 (1985), 4, 18.
[7]Ibid., p. 22.
[8]Sandra M. Gilbert and Susan Gubar, *The Madwoman In the Attic: The Woman Writer*

model's presumption that apparent inconsistencies in the narrative are due to unintended eruptions of repressed biographical material into the text. While Sadoff is more thorough and more sympathetic in her treatment of *Their Eyes Were Watching God* than, say, Robert Towers is in his treatment of *The Color Purple*, she presumes, as Towers does, that the author has inadvertently written something other than what she intended, and that what the author intended was an unironic and unambiguous realism, in Hurston's case the realism of the heterosexual romance plot that structured so many European and American novels about women in the eighteenth and nineteenth centuries.[9] Neither critic entertains the possibility that certain ostensible violations may be calculated subversions of conventions that the authors regarded as permeated with white, masculinist values or that other ostensible violations may arise from the fact that the authors were writing not realism but romance—perhaps in part because, unlike the genre of realism, the genre of romance is recognized as highly conventional, so that its ideological implications are easier both to underscore and to undermine.[10]

---

and the Nineteenth-Century Literary Imagination (New Haven: Yale University Press, 1979), especially pp. 46–53.

[9]Nancy Miller coined the phrase "heroines' texts" for such novels; see *The Heroine's Text: Readings in the French and English Novel, 1722–1782* (New York: Columbia University Press, 1980). Rachel Blau DuPlessis summarizes Miller's argument in her *Writing beyond the Ending: Narrative Strategies of Twentieth-Century Women Writers* (Bloomington: Indiana University Press, 1985), p. 15: " 'Story' for women has typically meant plots of seduction, courtship, the energies of quest deflected into sexual downfall, the choice of a marriage partner, the melodramas of beginning, middle, and end, the trajectories of sexual arousal and release." DuPlessis contends that twentieth-century narratives by women deliberately "rupture" traditional sequence or syntax in order to evade the closure imposed by such plots.

[10]The critical responses already mentioned suggest one reason that a writer concerned with revising encoded ideologies might have for avoiding realism. Despite the existence of a great deal of narrative theory establishing that the realist novel is as conventional in its premises and methods as the sonnet, the epic, or such "genre" novels as the detective story or the gothic—see for example David Lodge, *The Modes of Modern Fiction: Metaphor, Metonymy, and the Typology of Modern Literature* (Ithaca: Cornell University Press, 1977), especially pp. 22–41—realism is such a dominant form that its tacit claim to mirror reality is often difficult to question. More significant, the assumption that the realist novel is "like life" tends to imply that the rules governing this sort of novel come from a repository of dicta called "reality" and carry moral as well as metaphysical weight. Thus, to call a fictional outcome—say, a conclusion that redraws racial or gender boundaries—"unrealistic" is to suggest not only that things don't happen this way "in reality" (which may amount on examination to the observation that things have never happened this way before) but that the

Romance is a term with a wide range of applications, especially when contrasted to *realism*,[11] but it also has a more delimited technical sense that turns out to be surprisingly relevant to *The Color Purple* and illuminates certain analogous aspects of *Their Eyes Were Watching God*. Such late plays of Shakespeare as *The Tempest* and, especially, *The Winter's Tale*, which draw on pastoral for a number of their governing premises but go on to use these premises as means to develop a tragicomic plot, have striking affinities with the narrative strategies created by Walker and Hurston. Shakespearean romance can in certain respects serve as a structural paradigm for these two novels without necessarily standing in a relationship of direct influence to them or absorbing them into its own network of assumptions about how the world is structured and how human beings fit into this world.[12] Indeed, the romance paradigm seems most important in this context precisely because it formally encodes a system of hierarchical relations that have ideological repercussions, and because this recognizably conventional system of hierarchical relations is also the ideology of racism and patriarchy, which the two novels expose and, ultimately, invert.

I

In his introduction to the New Arden edition of *The Tempest*, Frank Kermode advances "pastoral tragi-comedy" as a more precise, if more cumbersome, designation for the late plays of Shakespeare more commonly termed romances.[13] The phrase is useful insofar as

---

rules of "reality" do not *allow* such developments, and therefore that they *ought* not to occur. In this way the mode of fictional realism becomes an arena for prescriptions based on a reading of ethics presumptively enjoined by something like a natural order.

[11]Richard Chase, in his classic study *The American Novel and Its Tradition* (Garden City, N.Y.: Doubleday/Anchor, 1957), distinguishes between "the romance, or romance-novel, and the novel proper," the former category including "that freer, daring, more brilliant fiction that contrasts with the solid moral inclusiveness and massive equability of the [nineteenth-century] English novel" (vii–viii).

[12]Walker was graduated from Sarah Lawrence College; Hurston, from Barnard College. Both read widely in several traditions. There is no reason to believe that either writer's desire to claim her black heritage precluded a canny reappropriation through re-vision of the white, patriarchal canon.

[13]Frank Kermode, Introduction to *The Tempest* (New York: Random House, 1964), p. liv.

it invokes the tradition of pastoral and thus a set of conventions celebrating a rural, "natural" community often explicitly identified with the nonwhite inhabitants of Africa or the New World and constituted in implicit opposition to a dominant urban community.[14] *The Color Purple* is clearly pastoral in these respects, for in it Walker makes a group of black farmers the central social unit and uses this community as a vantage point from which to deliver a blistering critique of the surrounding white culture. The denunciation is sometimes overt, as when Sofia fulminates: "They have the nerve to try to make us think slavery fell through because of us. . . . Like us didn't have sense enough to handle it. All the time breaking hoe handles and letting the mules loose in the wheat. But how anything they build can last a day is a wonder to me. They backward. . . . Clumsy, and unlucky."[15] More frequently, however, the white society figures as profoundly unnecessary, invisible for most of the action and appearing only as explosions of violence and insanity that sporadically intrude into the relatively intelligible world of the protagonists, as when the mayor's wife asks Sofia to be her maid and precipitates the beating, jailing, and domestic servitude of Sofia and the rape of Squeak or when the English engineers casually eradicate the Olinka village in the process of turning the jungle into a rubber plantation.

The point of view of pastoral is conventionally simple, artless and naïve—values rendered, of course, by means that are complex, subtle, and sophisticated—and can become the locus of a sustained attack on the mores of the mainstream society.[16] Walker's protagonist Celie (whose name by various etymologies means "holy," "healing," and "heavenly"), is in these respects an exemplary pastoral protag-

[14]Kermode, *English Pastoral Poetry: From the Beginnings to Marvell* (London: George G. Harrap, 1952), pp. 19, 40.

[15]Alice Walker, *The Color Purple* (New York: Washington Square Press, 1982), p. 100, hereafter cited parenthetically in the text. All of Sofia's dialogue is of course comprehended in the written "dialect" of Celie's letters to God, a point that Gates makes in observing, "In the speeches of her characters, Celie's voice and a character's merge into one, almost exactly as we saw happen in *Their Eyes* when Janie and her narrator speak in the merged voice of free indirect discourse. In these passages from *The Color Purple*, the distinction between mimesis and diagesis is apparently obliterated: the opposition between them has *collapsed*" ("Color Me Zora," p. 249).

[16]"This indeed is one of the assumptions of pastoral," observes William Empson, "that you can say everything about complex people by a complete consideration of simple people." *English Pastoral Poetry* (New York: Norton, 1938), p. 137.

onist, for her defining quality, and thus the defining quality of the narrative, is innocence. If this innocence subjects her to violation at the outset of the story, it also figures as a capacity for wonder and thus for experience. Celie learns, and as she learns her pastoral community develops, in a movement that implicitly restores a submerged Edenic ideal of harmony between individual human beings and between humanity and the natural order.

It is this development that makes *The Color Purple* a narrative—tragicomedy as well as pastoral—and provides striking affinities with the late Shakespearean romances. Kermode has defined romance as "a mode of exhibiting the action of magical and moral laws in a version of human life so selective as to obscure, for the special purpose of concentrating attention on these laws, the fact that in reality their force is intermittent and only fitfully glimpsed."[17] Certainly the moral laws of Walker's novel, subtitled in the original hard-cover edition *A Moral Tale*, have magical power, producing consequences that are not in naturalistic terms remotely credible. Nettie, Samuel, and the children miraculously return from the sea after their ship is reported missing, to provide a conclusion that brings together all the far-flung characters in a celebration that is part family reunion, part assertion of a new social order that will supplant the old (the celebration takes place on the Fourth of July, a date on which, as Harpo explains to a representative of the younger generation, white people are busy "celebrating they independence from England" and consequently black people "can spend the day celebrating each other" [p. 250]). Shortly before this climactic juncture, Shug returns from her last heterosexual fling to find Celie and Albert reconciled and living in platonic harmony, a reversal prompted by Albert's recognition that "meanness kill" (p. 201). Shortly before *this* development Celie inherits a house, a store, and the information that her children are not the product of incest. And this last windfall comes after the success of Celie's company, Folkspants, Ltd., an enterprise purveying androgyny to Depression-era black sharecroppers. The comic impetus of Walker's story is so powerful that it absorbs questions of probability and motivation. As

[17]Kermode, Introduction to *The Tempest*, liv.

Northrop Frye has noted of analogous Shakespearean plots, "What emerges at the end is not a logical consequence of the preceding action, as in tragedy, but something more like a metamorphosis."[18]
In Shakespearean romance the metamorphosis is both social and metaphysical. It is social in that it involves a redemptive conclusion absorbing all the principal characters, whether or not they seem to deserve redemption. Moreover, as J. H. P. Pafford observes in writing of *The Winter's Tale*, the element of tragedy in romances derives from the suffering characters must undergo because of the misbehavior of a powerful male figure; this figure nevertheless "always shares to the full in the final blessings, and, however guilty and responsible for the sufferings of others, he is ultimately absolved by facile excuse, if any is needed at all."[19] In *The Color Purple* the most important agent of suffering is also a (relatively) powerful male figure, Celie's husband Mr. ——, whose unarticulated name, in the manner of epistolary fictions since Richardson's *Pamela*, suggests fearful effacement of an identity too dangerous to reveal and whose transformation is signaled by a renaming that at once diminishes and humanizes.[20] In this case, the gratuitous absolution is also a conversion that affects descendants, for both Mr. —— (who is transformed into a little man given to collecting shells and called merely Albert) and his son, Harpo, are absolved by becoming integrated into a female-defined value community, "finding themselves" at last in the traditionally female roles of seamstress and housekeeper.

The metamorphoses of romance are not limited to the social order, and they have an analogous metaphysical dimension in *The Color Purple*, where Celie's progress also serves to redefine the proper relation between human beings and the natural world they inhabit.

[18]Northrop Frye, *A Natural Perspective: The Development of Shakespearean Comedy and Romance* (New York: Columbia University Press, 1965), pp. 123–24.
[19]J. H. P. Pafford, Introduction to Arden Shakespeare Edition of *The Winter's Tale* (London: Methuen, 1968), p. lxii.
[20]Frye notes that the comic drive is essentially directed toward identity. Insofar as this drive toward identity is an individual matter (rather than involving a whole society), it takes the form of "an awakening to self-knowledge, which is typically a release from a humor or a mechanical form of behavior" (*A Natural Perspective*, p. 118). It is interesting in this context to note that masculine brutality appears to be a "humor or mechanical form of behavior" in *The Color Purple*.

Shug's disquisitions on religion and on the behavior required by a redefined God are consonant with the pastoral's characteristic fusion of reverence and hedonism and with a long tradition that uses pastoral convention to attack the excesses and misconceptions of established religious practice.[21] "God love all them [sexual] feelings," Shug assures a scandalized Celie. "That's some of the best stuff God did," and she goes on to maintain, "God love admiration. . . . Not vain, just wanting to share a good thing" (p. 178). In the ensuing critique of prevailing religious beliefs, this undemanding God emerges as not only sexless—an "it" rather than a "he"—but also radically decentered: not one but many and in fact, according to Shug, "everything that is or ever was or ever will be. And when you can feel that, and be happy to feel that, you've found It" (p. 178). Like the value systems governing traditional romances, the nurturing pantheism this novel affirms as an ideal also figures implicitly as a preexisting state or Edenic norm that must be restored before human beings can attain social equilibrium. Celie only embraces it completely in the greeting of her last letter, which describes the celebratory reunion of all the principal characters: "Dear God. Dear stars, dear trees, dear sky, dear peoples. Dear Everything. Dear God" (p. 249).[22]

Finally, Shakespearean romances provide precedent and rationale for an aspect of *The Color Purple* that readers have found particularly anomalous, the "Africa" passages, which in effect disrupt the Amer-

---

[21]The most famous attack on religious excesses and misconceptions in English pastoral occurs in Milton's "Lycidas." In *The Oaten Flute: Essays on Pastoral Poetry and the Pastoral Ideal* (Cambridge: Harvard University Press, 1975), Renato Poggioli suggests that even in its most orthodox Christian manifestations the pastoral ideal is based on "a double longing after innocence and happiness" and ultimately "stands at the opposite pole from the Christian one, even if it believes with the latter that the lowly will be exalted and that the only bad shepherds are the shepherds of men" (p. 1). Kermode points to the Renaissance pastoral as a site where Neoplatonism could systematize "the relation between spiritual and physical love and beauty," and the *Song of Solomon* "provided all the necessary authority for expressing mystical love in erotic imagery" (*English Pastoral Poetry*, p. 35).

[22]Poggioli remarks that utopias constitute "after all . . . the idyll of the future," the pastoral Eden made the terminus of the narrative instead of the origin (*The Oaten Flute*, pp. 28–29). Frye similarly argues that in Shakespearean romance the return to Eden or a golden age is "a vision of something never seen or experienced, and hence, when it is presented as something we return to, it is a genuinely new vision" (*A Natural Perspective*, pp. 132–33).

ican action for some forty pages, when a whole cache of withheld letters from Nettie is suddenly revealed. These letters detail the story of Nettie's adoption by a missionary family and her subsequent travels to New York, England, Senegal, Liberia, and finally the unnamed country of the Olinka. In the Olinka village she recapitulates Celie's discoveries, decrying the irrationality of the sex-gender system, becoming increasingly committed to the nonhuman, asexual God, and achieving a heterosexual version of Celie's stable, loving relationship. The function of the "Africa" section is clearly to provide analogies and contrasts to the dominant action. In this function, as in its seeming violation of realist conventions, it parallels scenes in the romances taking place in what Frye has called the "green world," a pastoral landscape that serves as a "symbol of natural society, the word natural referring to the original human society which is the proper home of man" and is "associated with things which in the context of the ordinary world seem unnatural, but which are in fact attributes of nature as a miraculous and irresistible reviving power."[23] This "green world" is "particularly the world in which the heroine . . . dies and comes back to life,"[24] and as such it is the locus of Nettie's reincarnation as correspondent and conarrator.

The village of the Olinka, with its organically round huts, its roof-leaf religion, its restorative myths of black hegemony, and its simple agrarian economy, is in some respects, and especially initially, an idyllic counter to the world that Celie must dismantle and remake. In its geographical distance from the world of the main action, in the length of time the daughter-heroine spends there (as missing and presumed dead), in its structural function of healing old wounds through a marriage and the founding of a family, and in its recapitulation of major themes of the containing drama, this generic "Africa" most resembles the Bohemia of *The Winter's Tale*—with one signal difference. Whereas Perdita in *The Winter's Tale* learns from the pastoral Bohemia, which in many respects remains an ideal, Nettie in *The Color Purple* ends up criticizing the Olinka society, which she first perceives as a natural and self-determining black community but soon finds sexist and fatally vulnerable to incursions

[23]Frye, *A Natural Perspective*, pp. 142–43.
[24]Ibid., 145.

by the encompassing white empire. By contrast, Celie's world becomes more woman-centered and more self-sufficient as it develops, finally containing and assimilating even elements of the white community in the person of Sofia's former charge, Miss Eleanor Jane, who leaves her own home to work for Sofia.

But this one difference in many ways completely inverts the emphasis of the romance, suggesting the extent to which Walker unsettles this structural paradigm in the process of applying it. As a marginal and marginalizing work, *The Color Purple* not only reveals the central preoccupations of the tradition within which it locates itself but succeeds in turning a number of these preoccupations inside out, at once exposing the ideology that informs them and insinuating the alternative meanings that, by insisting on its own centrality, the paradigm has suppressed.

II

One of the chief preoccupations of romance as a genre is the relation between men and women. *The Winter's Tale*, which, in this as in other respects, is the closest structural analogue to *The Color Purple*, deals with the unmotivated jealousy and cruelty of a man who is also a ruler, his loss of his wife and daughter for a period of sixteen years, and their restoration (both had been preserved in "green worlds")[25] after he atones and comes to terms with his own misdeeds. The restoration is bittersweet: on the one hand, time has elapsed and many opportunities are gone for good; on the other hand, a young central couple restores the succession and suggests a more humane and rational future, both for this family and for the state that they govern.

Allowing for the fact that in *The Color Purple* the female roles of mother, daughter, wife, and lover are slippery to the point of being interchangeable, the plot of *The Winter's Tale* has clear affinities with the plot of *The Color Purple*—and a very different focus. Despite the attention given to the main female characters, the play is *about* the

[25]Frye identifies Paulina's chapel, where Hermione hides for an unimaginable sixteen years, as the corollary to Perdita's Bohemia. It is worth noting that if this is the case, the pastoral quality of this particular green world derives largely from the fact that all its inhabitants are female.

father and ruler, Leontes, about his crime, his punishment, and his eventual, though partial, restitution. By analogy *The Color Purple* ought to be about Mr. ——, about *his* crime, punishment and eventual restitution. And of course Mr. —— goes through all these stages, emerging at the conclusion as an integral part of the new society embodied in the family that surrounds him. But *The Color Purple* is not his story. This point is especially important in view of the fact that Steven Spielberg seized on the underlying romance structure of Walker's novel when he made it into a film; he reinscribed Mr. —— (whom he renamed simply Mister, so that the title of authority became this character's identity) at the center of the story, making his change of heart the turning point of the action and involving him in supplementary scenes that show him coming to reembrace his estranged family. Even more striking, Spielberg went on to reinscribe the law of the father exactly where Walker had effaced it, by providing Shug with a textually gratuitous "daddy," who is also a preacher and thus the representative of the Christian white father-God explicitly repudiated in the passage that gives the book its title.[26] This father asserts his power by refusing to *speak* to Shug until she and all the inhabitants of the evolving new society who have gathered in the alternative structure of the juke joint are themselves assimilated to the Christian church and give *voice* to Christian hymns. Spielberg's restorative instinct here was unerring, for Walker uses the Afro-American motif of "finding a voice" primarily to decenter patriarchal authority, giving speech to hitherto muted women, who change meanings in the process of articulating and thus appropriating the dominant discourse. Spielberg replaced this entire narrative tendency with its reverse, not only restoring voice to the father but making paternal words uniquely efficacious: the film's Mister is shown visiting Washington, talking to bureaucrats, and in substance becoming the agent of the climactic reunion between Celie and Nettie.[27]

---

[26]"Then she tell me this old white man is the same God she used to see when she prayed. If you wait to find God in church, Celie, she say, that's who is bound to show up, cause that's where he live.... Cause that's the one that's in the white folks' white bible" (p. 177).

[27]Scott McMillin reminds me that, paradoxically, Spielberg's additions are often powerful precisely inasmuch as they make patriarchal speech a *visual* phenomenon:

In the novel, on the other hand, the emphasis is skewed away from this male discovery of identity. If Albert and Harpo "find themselves," it is within a context of redefinition that not only denies male privilege but ultimately denies that the designations "male" and "female" are meaningful bases for demarcating difference. In a fictional universe governed by the written "dialect" of Celie and initially conditioned by the paternal injunction *"You better not never tell nobody but God. It'd kill your mammy"* (p. 11), speech among women turns out to be revivifying rather than death-dealing, especially inasmuch as such speech has the potential to bring about romance's characteristic reconstitution of society.

The reconstitution of society is largely a matter of redefinition, presented as the inevitable corollary of taking seriously the view from underneath, not only figuratively but also literally. For example, Celie's detached description of heterosexual intercourse, which prompts Shug to observe, "You make it sound like he going to the toilet on you" (p. 79), leads her into a revisionary discusion of female anatomy:

> You never enjoy it at all? she ast, puzzle. Not even with your children daddy?
> Never, I say.
> Why Miss Celie, she say, you still a virgin.
> What? I ast.
> Listen, she say, right down there in your pussy is a little button that gits real hot when you do you know what with somebody. It git hotter and hotter and then it melt. That the good part. But other parts good too, she say. Lot of sucking go on, here and there, she say. Lot of finger and tongue work.
> Button? Finger and *tongue*? My face hot enough to melt itself. [p. 79]

Mister's plot-advancing words are not *heard*, but are presented in a series of dumb-show vignettes. Furthermore, Mister does not speak at the concluding celebration; his Jaques-like self-exclusion from the reunion (which requires him to occupy a separate frame, as he stands alone in the middle of a sunset-stained field) evokes instead the American icon of isolate and taciturn masculinity, withdrawing from the din of female society to light out for the territories or ride off into that sunset. Walker's own character, Albert, is unremarkable at the conclusion of the novel because he belongs—he is *absorbed* into the buzzing, blooming female community.

Shug begins by replacing conventional terminology for the female genitals, shifting emphasis from the lack or hole of patriarchal representation to a "little button" that "git hotter and hotter and then it melt"—a mixed metaphor from the point of view of the dominant discursive practice, which of course has only recently begun to acknowledge the existence of buttons that behave in this way. The consequence is immediately clear to Celie: if the important organ is not a hole but a button, then stimulation can come from such androgynous appendages as "finger and tongue," and intercourse is not only insufficient but unnecessary for female sexual pleasure. Shug's redefinition of the word "virgin" in this passage is equally threatening to patriarchal control over women's bodies, in that it places priority not on penetration, and thus on the social mechanism for guaranteeing ownership of children, but on enjoyment, making the woman's own response the index of her "experience" (p. 79).

In the development of the story, Celie, along with the appositely named Squeak, acquires a voice and becomes a producer of meanings, while Shug and Sofia, articulate all along, increase their authority until it is evident that female voices have the power to dismantle hierarchical oppositions that ultimately oppress everyone and to create a new order in which timeworn theories about male and female "natures" vanish because they are useless for describing the qualities of people. Near the conclusion, the transformed Mr. ——, now happily calling himself only Albert, tries to explain his admiration for Shug: "To tell the truth, Shug act more manly than most men. I mean she upright, honest. Speak her mind and the devil take the hindmost." But Celie takes issue with these categories. "Harpo not like this, I tell him. You not like this. What Shug got is womanly it seem like to me. Specially since she and Sofia the ones that got it." Albert continues to worry the problem—"Sofia and Shug not like men . . . but they not like women either"—until Celie makes the relevant distinction: "You mean they not like you or me." (p. 236) On the basis of such redrawn lines the entire immediate society reconstitutes itself, in the manner of Shakespearean romance, around a central couple. This couple is not only black, it is aging and lesbian. Yet clearly Celie and Shug are intended to suggest the nucleus of a new and self-sustaining society: the triply marginalized become center and source.

III

The issue of voice—and especially of voice as a way of appropriating discourse and remaking meanings—returns this discussion to the writer whom Walker has repeatedly claimed as her "foremother," Zora Neale Hurston, and to *Their Eyes Were Watching God*, in which the protagonist, Janie, discovers her voice and uses it to assert her own authority in a world full of speechmakers and tale-tellers. Janie's voice, first muted by the pathos of her Nanny's stories, emerges to threaten her first husband but then is subsumed to the "big voice" of Jody Starks until the moment of the insult that by the logic of the narrative kills him: "Humph! Talkin' bout *me* lookin' old! When you pull down yo' britches, you look lak de change uh life" (p. 123). Janie's relationship with Tea Cake reinforces the association of language and sexual potency—"He done taught me de maiden language all over," Janie tells her best friend Phoeby (p. 173)—and finally raises her to a level of equality that is to some extent both sexual and narrative, for in "the muck," the fertile Florida bottomland where Tea Cake takes her, "she could listen and laugh and even talk some herself if she wanted to. She got so she could tell big stories herself from listening to the rest" (p. 200).

"The muck" in this novel plays the role of a "green world" in Shakespearean romance: it is a magical, somehow "more natural" realm that shapes both the outside world and the conclusion toward which the narrative tends. Tea Cake describes it in unmistakably pastoral terms: "Folks don't do nothin' down dere but make money and fun and foolishness" (p. 192), and the narrator elaborates: "Pianos living three lifetimes in one. Blues made and used right on the spot. Dancing, fighting, singing, crying, laughing, winning and losing love every hour. Work all day for money, fight all night for love. The rich black earth clinging to bodies and biting the skin like ants"(p. 197). Precisely because "the muck" is a "green world," however, it represents a transitory stage in Janie's passage toward achieving her own identity, a passage that the romance paradigm further implies will lead to achieving the basis for a reconstituted society. The heterosexual idyll with Tea Cake is thus not the culmination of the plot but a transformative moment that leads to the culmination. In other words, the theme of finding a voice does not supplement the heterosexual romance plot of *Their Eyes Were Watching God* but supplants that plot, just as the story of Janie's *telling* her story frames and in framing displaces the ostensible main story of Janie's quest for heterosexual love.

The action of *Their Eyes Were Watching God* begins with a homecoming, but against the evidence the Eatonville residents eagerly collect—the "overhalls" that Janie wears[28] and her manifestly mateless state—this is a triumphal return. The whole of the ensuing narrative aims to establish that triumph, displayed especially in the significance of Janie's ability to tell her own story. The capacity to tell this story rests on two conditions. The first is that there be a story to tell, a plot, a completed action in Aristotle's terms. But because a completed action is one that has ended, the quest for heterosexual love must terminate in order to be appropriated by discourse, and the only terminus that will preserve the fulfillment of the quest while imposing closure on it is the apparently tragic one of Tea Cake's death. Rather paradoxically, then, the killing of Tea Cake becomes part of the larger *comic* impetus that establishes Janie's voice and gives him a fictional "life" that she can possess wholly: "Of course he wasn't dead. He could never be dead until she herself had finished feeling and thinking. The kiss of memory made pictures of love and light against the wall. Here was peace" (p. 286).

The appropriative move goes further. In appropriating Tea Cake in the form of her story, Janie brings the "horizons" so important in the development of her aspirations—she undertook her "journey to the horizons in search of *people*" (p. 138)—back to Eatonville, the black community that functions as the locus of black storytelling in this novel. "Ah done been tuh de horizon and back and now Ah kin sit heah in mah house and live by comparisons," she tells Phoeby

---

[28]Miriam Amihai has pointed out to me that Hurston's female hero, who not only wears the pants (and very proletarian pants at that) but looks sexy in them (to the Eatonville onlookers Janie looks as if she has two grapefruits in her hip pockets), doubtless inspired Walker to base Celie's economic independence on the cottage industry that produces unisex but provocatively sexual trousers.

(p. 284), but the closing image of the narrative affirms that the horizon has come with her: "She pulled in her horizon like a great fish-net. Pulled it from around the waist of the world and draped it over her shoulder. So much of life in its meshes! She called in her soul to come and see" (p. 286). And this looping, "netting" action also contains the novel, which begins at the end of Janie's story and comes back to it, drawing the whole "life" of the plot in its meshes.[29]

The central action of *Their Eyes Were Watching God* is thus Janie's telling of her story, and the climax of this central action is the pulling in of the horizon, a dramatization of the fact of closure that establishes Janie as an accomplished storyteller. If one condition of this action is a completed story that can be told, a second condition is an audience capable of hearing it. Janie's privileged listener is her best friend, Phoeby, whose credentials as audience are her empathy and equality with the narrator, to the point of being at least potentially interchangeable with her. "You can tell 'em what Ah say if you wants to," Janie assures her. "Dat's just the same as me 'cause mah tongue is in mah friend's mouf" (p. 17). The image implies that the relation of female narrator to female audience is nonhegemonic and reversible. But like so many of the images associated with storytelling in this book it is also highly sexual, suggesting further that the narratorial couple composed of Janie and Phoeby has displaced the heterosexual couple as the desired union that motivates and finally terminates the action. The commencement of Janie's "conscious life" dates from a revelation in which the spectacle of bees fertilizing the blossoms of a pear tree led to the conclusion "So this was a marriage!" (pp. 23–24), but Janie's subsequent three marriages somewhat miraculously produce no children.[30] The real fertilization seems to occur when Janie combines with Phoeby to give birth to her story after she has returned to Eatonville, the town of tale-tellers. This story addresses the values governing her community, its misplaced emphasis on possession, status, class, and sexual hierarchy, all legacies of its founder Jody Starks. In narrating, Janie moves to

[29]Fishing is also one of the activities asserting Janie's egalitarian relation to Tea Cake: Phoeby announces at the end of Janie's story, "Ah means tuh make Sam take me fishin' wid him after this" (p. 284). And fishing itself is an exemplary pastoral activity. For "piscatory" as a subgenre of pastoral, see Poggioli, p. 7.

[30]A point underscored in the version developed by *The Color Purple*, where the consequence of heterosexual activity for women is almost invariably "getting big."

renovate the society that she has rejoined, transforming it at last into a female speech community embracing the playful, nonhierarchical values that constitute the lesson she draws from her experience—an Edenville.[31]

Walker clearly picks up on these implications in her own revision of *Their Eyes Were Watching God*. In *The Color Purple* a homosexual romance plot replaces the heterosexual one, with the appetizing Tea Cake ("So you sweet as all dat?" Janie inquires when she learns his name [p. 149]) transformed into Celie's lover and mentor Sugar Avery. Moreover, the drama of Celie's epistolary self-creation revolves around the discovery of a female audience that finally fulfills the ideal of co-respondence. Celie initially writes to God as an alternative to speech. The process of finding her speaking voice is a process of finding her audience, first in Sofia, then in Shug, but she is not able to deliver the Old Testament–style curse that in turn delivers her from bondage until she is assured of the existence of Nettie, her ideal audience, who also tells a story leading to identical conclusions about the nature of spiritual and social reality—as if her sister's tongue were in her mouth.

IV

Thus in *Their Eyes Were Watching God*, Hurston's ostensible frame tale decenters what it appears to comprehend, shifting the story of heterosexual love to the margin even as it contains and completes that story. It behaves, that is, like the frame or margin that Jacques Derrida has discussed under the rubric of the *parergon*. Conventionally extrinsic, supplementary, or inessential to that which it borders, a parergon is simultaneously intrinsic and essential, inasmuch as the priority of the center depends entirely on the oppositional

[31]Eatonville is a real community, founded by (among others) Hurston's own father; see Alice Walker, "Zora Neale Hurston: A Cautionary Tale and a Partisan View," in *In Search of Our Mothers' Gardens: Womanist Prose* (New York: Harvest/HBJ, 1983), p. 85. But even the names of real towns are sometimes the product of just this sort of highly literary slippage. For example Pysht, in the state of Washington, was christened out of a postal clerk's misreading. The town was to have been called Psyche, and to have been companion to a town that did receive its intended name, Sappho. Minority communities, like minority texts, appear particularly subject to mainstream misreadings.

relation of center to margin. Yet to call attention to this margin is to destroy its marginality, for the parergon is what it is by virtue of "disappearing, sinking in, obliterating itself, dissolving just as it expends its greatest energy."[32] To call attention to the margin is to render it no longer marginal and consequently to collapse the center in a general unsettling of oppositional hierarchies.

This turning of attention to what is not conventionally in the center—most obviously to conventionally marginal characters—is of course a characteristic activity of conventionally marginal writers: black women, for example. And of course to give voice to marginality—to let the margins *speak*—is to mix a metaphor intolerably, for a speaking margin cannot be a margin at all and in fact threatens to marginalize what has hitherto been perceived as the center.[33] Or, rather, such a phenomenon tends to destabilize precisely the hierarchical oppositions that give margin and center clearly demarcated meanings.

Such hierarchical oppositions are the basis of traditional genres. In the paradigm of the Shakespearean romance they guarantee the distinction between major and minor characters, between dominant and peripheral lines of action, and between classes, sexes, and generations—all of which may become confused during the development of the plot but must be sorted out so as to fall into place in a conclusion that at once reconciles apparently conflicting elements and confirms their inherent differences: the ritual marriage. This conclusion makes its model of unity the patriarchal family and its model of continuity the order of succession in which power passes from father to son. Distinctions of class, gender, and generation coincide with distinctions between major and minor, dominant and peripheral, on the levels of character and plot. These distinctions

[32]Jacques Derrida, "The Parergon," *October* 9 (Summer 1979), 35, 26. See also Marian Hobson, "Derrida's Scroll-Work," *Oxford Literary Review* 4, no. 3 (1981), 94–102.

[33]Philip Brian Harper aligns the parergonal "positing of the margin as essential" with the decentering of the postmodern subject and suggests "the supposed postmodernist 'decentering of the subject' [is] merely a symptom of the recentering of subjectivities which have traditionally been relegated to the borders—of texts, of works of art in general, of societies—as mere parerga to the dominant subjectivity whose hegemony itself has so long skewed our view of the relation between center and margin." "The Recentered Subject: *Pale Fire* and the Question of Marginality" (Unpublished paper, Cornell University), pp. 2–3.

are unalterable, a premise that becomes the basis for both the tragic and the comic aspects of pastoral tragicomedy.

But these distinctions are destabilized in *Their Eyes Were Watching God* and *The Color Purple*, novels that Rachel Blau DuPlessis has identified as employing a "narrative strategy of the multiple individual," in which the female hero "encompasses opposites and can represent both sociological debate and a psychic interplay between boundaries and boundlessness" and eventually "fuses with a complex and contradictory group; her power is articulated in and continued through a community that is formed in direct answer to the claims of love and romance."[34] Not only is the traditional heterosexual couple supplanted as emphasis of the action, but it is replaced by interchangeable versions of the same-sex couple: mother and daughter, sisters, lovers, narrator and audience. The roles of the characters have become slippery and permeable.

Perhaps most significant, the mother-daughter relation is continuously transformed. Dianne Sadoff observes the extent to which both novels suppress or overtly repudiate traditional mothering—Janie hates her Nanny and produces a story with Phoeby rather than children in any of her three marriages; Celie loses her children, and their foster-mother subsequently dies—and suggests that such suppressions or repudiations "question anxiety-free matrilineage."[35] The issue is particularly important in light of the role of literary foremother that Walker has assigned to Hurston, and Sadoff uses what she perceives as an unacknowledged theme of failed mothering within the two novels to bolster readings that discern "ruptures" within *Their Eyes* and "scars of concealment" within *The Color Purple*, with its imbedded claims of unproblematic descent from the mother tale.

But the preceding discussion of the two novels might suggest, rather, that the issue is less one of the failure of mothering than of a redefinition, in which mothering is presented as a wholly relational activity. In *The Color Purple* children create mothers by circulating among women who in other contexts are daughters, sisters, friends, wives, and lovers. Celie's children pass first to Corrine, then to Nettie. Squeak takes on Sofia's children when Sofia goes to jail, and

[34]DuPlessis, *Writing beyond the Ending*, p. 142.
[35]Sadoff, "Black Matrilineage," p. 25.

Sofia later mothers Squeak's daughter Suzie Q and—with exasperated acknowledgment that even unwilling nurture can engender filial affection—the white girl Eleanor Jane. And Celie's love affair with Shug begins from an erotic exchange that is poignantly figured as a mutual reparenting: "Then I feels something real soft and wet on my breast, feel like one of my little lost babies mouth. Way after while, I act like a little lost baby too" (p. 109).

In *Their Eyes Were Watching God*, mothering is intimately allied with production of a powerful narrative that enjoins a world view and a series of prescriptions about how to live. Nanny's story of Janie's lineage, which begins from what appears to be a piece of maternal wisdom, "De nigger woman is de mule uh de world so fur as Ah can see" (p. 29), concludes with the demand that Janie marry the man who, in Hurston's wonderfully apt conflation of social class and phallic power, owns "de onliest organ in town" (p. 41). While Janie ultimately repudiates this version of her story as unlivable, her repudiation is explicitly dissociated from an agonistic Oedipal model in which the child kills the parental figure in order to revise this parent's master narrative.[36] If the narrative logic by which an ensuing action is figured as a consequent action[37] indicates that Janie is responsible for the death of two husbands, the same logic makes Nanny's death the consequence of her *own* story, for Nanny's acknowledgement that she is dying, "Put me down easy, Janie, Ah'm a cracked plate," occurs at the end of the narrative in which she coerces Janie into marrying Logan Killicks (p. 37). In replacing Nanny's story about sexual oppression with an alternative story about sexual love that paradoxically enables her to live independently and alone—"by comparisons" (p. 284)—Janie in effect takes on the maternal function, in company of course with her listener, Phoeby. She becomes author of her own story, both source and subject of maternal wisdom, in effect giving birth to herself.

[36]This is of course the (masculine) model of influence introduced by Harold Bloom in *The Anxiety of Influence* (New York: Oxford University Press, 1973).

[37]Narrative tends to insinuate more causal links than we are allowed to infer from sequences in daily life; to construe "the king died and then the queen died" as "the queen died *because* the king had died" is both an informal fallacy and an orthodox reader response that makes a plot out of mere sequence. In narrative, post hoc is likely to be propter hoc, unless the causal interpretation is expressly ruled out.

Clearly in Walker's and Hurston's novels mothers are no guarantors of succession or legitimacy, and mothering is a slippery and even reversible relationship. Furthermore, Walker has suggested that the same sort of observation holds for literary motherhood among black women writers. Indeed, in her essay "In Search of Our Mothers' Gardens" she elides the distinction between biological and literary motherhood in the same way that in *The Color Purple* she elides the distinction between mothering and other, conventionally contrary female functions. Mothers are artists, artistic precursors are mothers, and in either case the mother's creation may be inseparable from the daughter's: perhaps Phillis Wheatley's mother "herself was a poet—though only her daughter's name is signed to the poems we know."[38] This collaborative model of maternal influence suggests a subversively extended family romance, in which the mother as cocreator is simultaneously parent of the writer and her lover or spouse. Most disruptive for the absolute status of all these role definitions, she may even become the daughter of her own daughter. Du Plessis has suggested that in fulfilling or completing her biological mother's work the twentieth-century woman writer is inclined to dramatize her mother's situation, recreating her mother as a character and revising her destiny by reinscribing it in the fiction.[39] Alice Walker, who gave birth to her stepmother when she created Celie,[40] also uses *The Color Purple* to revise her relation to the woman she has elsewhere called her foremother. Gates points out that the photograph of Hurston parenthetically described in Walker's essay "Zora Neale Hurston: A Cautionary Tale and a Partisan View"—"(I have a photograph of her in pants, boots, and broadbrim that was given to me by her brother, Everette. She has her foot up on the running board of a car—presumably hers, and bright red—and looks racy)"—is in essence the photograph of Shug Avery that fascinates

[38]Walker, "In Search of Our Mothers' Gardens," in Walker, *In Search of Our Mothers' Gardens*, p. 243.

[39]DuPlessis, *Writing beyond the Ending*, pp. 93–94.

[40]She has captioned a photograph in *The Alice Walker Calendar for 1986* "My mother, 'Miss Mary,' my stepmother Rachel ('Celie'), and my mother's mother Nettie" (New York: Harvest/HBJ, 1985), n.p. And Gates cites a personal letter from Walker reporting, "All names in *Purple* are *family* or Eatonton, Georgia, community names. . . . The germ for Celie is Rachel, my stepmother: she of the poem 'Burial' in *Revolutionary Petunias*" (*Signifying*, p. 280, n. 14).

Celie in *The Color Purple*: "I see her there in furs. Her face rouge. Her hair like somethin tail. She grinning with her foot on somebody motocar" (p. 16).[41] In recreating her relationship to Hurston as a reciprocal and interactive one, Walker dramatizes Hurston's literary role as the undoer of inessential and divisive hierarchies. In casting Hurston as Shug, she revises theories of influence as they apply to black women.

What is finally at stake in readings of the two novels is the centrality of the paradigms and values informing what mainstream Western society chooses to call literature. To invoke these paradigms and values as if they exhausted the possibilities, and to castigate Walker and Hurston for failure to realize them, is to judge according to assumptions rather like those of the white community that Sofia ridicules in *The Color Purple*. It is like maintaining that slavery failed because blacks didn't have sense enough to handle it. In this chapter I have suggested, on the contrary, that by treating the marginal as central and thereby unsettling the hierarchical relations that structure "mainstream" genres, Walker and Hurston manage to handle very well the conventions that threaten to enslave them in a system of representation not of their own making.

[41]Walker, "Zora Neale Hurston," *In Search of Our Mothers' Gardens*, p. 88. Gates compares the passages in "Color Me Zora," p. 254.

Chapter 4
Other Side, Other Woman:
Lady Oracle

Like *The Golden Notebook*, Margaret Atwood's 1976 novel *Lady Oracle* is acutely aware of its own status within the problematic category of "women's writing." Unlike *The Golden Notebook*, however, *Lady Oracle* plays at being representative of the most popular, and the most popularly maligned, tendencies in this category, in that its narrative mode from the outset is "confessional" in overtly mass-market terms. From the beginning, Joan Foster operates with the avowed intention of telling *her* side of the story, a story that by implication has already been told—badly, erroneously, mislead-ingly. Her aim, in the best "confessional" tradition, is to tell it "as she sees it," as it appears "through her own eyes." But in telling the other side, she is immediately implicated in describing her own situation under the gaze of others: of the people who variously constitute her according to their own requirements. The other side of her story is the story of her construction by others, who estrange her inasmuch as they occupy their own side, consolidating them-selves as dominant by isolating her as outcast.

The phrase "other side" first occurs in *Lady Oracle* when the ad-olescent Joan begins attending the quasi-religious services at the Jordan Chapel, and in this context designates a community of be-nevolent and vaguely protective ghosts. Joan, however, immediately recognizes the vulnerability inherent in becoming the object of even such spiritual mass scrutiny:

I read two of the hymns, at random. One was about a joyous boat ride across a river to the Other Side, where loved ones were awaiting. The other was about the blessed spirits of those who've gone before, watching o'er us for our safety till we reach the other shore. This thought made me uncomfortable. Being told in Sunday school that God was watching you every minute of every hour had been bad enough, but now I had to think about all those other people I didn't even know who were spying on me.[1]

Here, as elsewhere, the view from Joan's side inevitably amounts to a vision of *being* "spied on." The side from which others watch and judge her is inevitably the side that puts *her* in the position of Other. In such applications of the metaphor of "sides," the emphasis falls on the enormity of the gap between self and others. For instance, in the opening of the novel Joan regretfully imagines an ad hoc community made up of the people from whom she has fled, all of them now inhabitants of an unattainable other side: "I closed my eyes: there in front of me, across an immense stretch of blue which I recognized as the Atlantic Ocean, was everyone I had left on the other side. On a beach, of course; I'd seen a lot of Fellini movies. The wind rippled their hair, they smiled and waved and called to me, though of course I couldn't hear the words" (p. 5). Although the Fellini paradigm (the reference is most obviously to *8½*) gives this scene a sort of benignant dottiness, the same paradigm emphasizes the alienation of Joan from the group she has envisioned. No matter how affectionately its members appear to regard her, they are too far away to include her. Later Joan returns to the Felliniesque beach to record her nostalgia for her husband, Arthur, and the separating ocean becomes the passage of time: "the future swept over us and we were separated. . . . He was moving at an ever-increasing speed away from me, into the land of the dead, the dead past, irretrievable" (pp. 148–49). The vast and unbridgeable nature of the distance between herself and the others finally counters the appearance of affection, becoming a figure first for estrangement and then for opposition. The most important illustration of this tendency is again her relationship with Arthur, which begins with his high-minded lack of interest in any of the activities of her daily

[1]Margaret Atwood, *Lady Oracle* (New York: Avon, 1976), p. 115, hereafter cited parenthetically in the text.

life, to the point where he is ignorant both that Joan spends her days writing "costume Gothics" and that she supports them both by doing so, then moves to his embarrassment when she becomes a publicly renowned "poetess" whose productions may cause people to think badly of him, then moves again to the suggestion of active menace when she begins to receive anonymous threats. But Arthur is to a certain extent only the most prominent of the male or male-identified others in *Lady Oracle* who stand in opposition to Joan and who ignore, reduce, or rewrite her life to fit more socially sanctioned stories.

The presence of such isolating and estranging versions of the Other Side within the novel is one of the factors tending to subvert the most common reading of the novel, a reading that Joan herself seems eager to advance at certain points. This reading in effect reduces her long and intricately structured narrative to a psychological and moral fable, rooting all the conflicts of the story in her own inability or unwillingness to make separations and take sides. According to this intepretation, the signal problem leading to all other conflicts is her own failure to make the key distinction between self and other, a distinction that originates and is summed up in the distinction between self and *mother*. As Joan observes late in the story, she has "carried [her] mother around [her] neck like a rotting albatross" all her life (p. 238), and the admission is presumed to bring her to the point where she can choose individuation of a rather radical sort: "I would never be able to make her happy. Or anyone else. Maybe it was time for me to stop trying" (p. 363). This decision, when read as an efficacious declaration of independence from the obligation to make anyone happy, is seen as resolving the initial problem of inadequate individuation that has led her to create and sustain false selves modeled on the heroines of Gothic romance, all of whom she has been inclined to conflate with the real one. The resolution is regarded as especially therapeutic because confusion about the true borders of the self was ultimately manifested as an incapacity to differentiate among the worlds of fantasy, fiction, dream, and hallucination, on one side, and reality, on the other.

Rather paradoxically, this construction of the story requires that Joan obey her own self-admonishments "pull yourself together" and "contain yourself" by cutting herself down to size, identifying and getting rid of the false selves that act as surface excrescences and so peeling down to a presumptive core of authenticity. Analogously, this construction of the story requires the *reader* to pull the novel together by identifying and separating out the false portions: by assigning parts of the narrative to the "real" fictional world, parts to the "fictions" imbedded within the fiction, and parts to uncontrolled aspects of Joan's imagination—as Joan's dreams, hallucinations, or fantasies-out-of-control.[2]

By now, of course, this sort of reading ought to sound suspiciously pat as well as suspiciously familiar. To sketch only two of the most obvious problems, first, the kernel "self" that it presumes to be lurking underneath veils of imaginative falsity is at once so simple and so impervious to influence from the surrounding mass culture (a culture depicted in minute and hilarious detail) that it seems theoretically indebted to the paperbacks on popular psychology sharing the supermarket display racks with the "costume Gothics" that are explored and parodied in *Lady Oracle*. This psychologizing of the plot—an operation in which social inequities are reinscribed as conflicts *within* the same "self" that would otherwise be perceived as the victim of these inequities—is of course a familiar strategy for translating the political issues of gender oppression into the realm of self-help. Second, some of the values assumed by this kind of interpretation seem open to further question insofar as the incidents

---

[2]See especially Sharon R. Wilson, "The Fragmented Self in *Lady Oracle*," *Commonwealth Novel in English* 1 (January 1982), 50–85, where Joan is a "narcissistic personality" in opposition to a psychologically constructed (if nowhere present in Atwood's narrative) "normal self"; Frank Davey, *Margaret Atwood: A Feminist Poetics* (Vancouver, B.C.: Talonbooks, 1984), where *Lady Oracle* is "the story of how [Joan's] projections of Gothic malevolence and glamour onto everyday reality have prevented her from seeing the actual rewards and dangers of everyday" (p. 59); Sherrill Grace, *Violent Duality: A Study of Margaret Atwood* (Montreal: Vehicule Press, 1980), where "it *may* be true . . . that all literature comes from other literature . . . but life does not, or should not, especially if that literature is Gothic romance" (p. 118, Grace's italics); Clara Thomas, "*Lady Oracle*: The Narrative of a Fool-Heroine," in *The Art of Margaret Atwood: Essays in Criticism*, ed. Arnold E. Davidson and Cathy N. Davidson (Toronto: Anansi Press, 1981), where Joan is "self-destructive" and must be educated "into individual and social responsibility" (p. 159); Catherine Sheldrick Ross, " 'Banished to This Other Place': Atwood's *Lady Oracle*," *English Studies in Canada* 6 (Winter 1980), where a strong analysis of structural analogues between frame and imbedded levels of plot is naturalized by being referred to "dangerous delusions" in which "Joan has been taken over by her shadowy twin" (pp. 469–70).

to which they are supposed to apply occur within a work of fiction. For example, the *creation* of fictions becomes in this context a debased and unhealthy activity, both because it manufactures false selves and worlds, which must then be discriminated from the real or true ones, and because it is is associated with a lack of self-control: Joan's trancelike state when she touch-types her "costume Gothics" is a case in point. While *Lady Oracle* incorporates elements of many genres, it is certainly a *Kunstlerroman*, a portrait of the artist as a young woman, and as such resists the unequivocal privileging of a "real self" when one implied opposite is the persona created by the imagination and of a "real world" when one implied opposite is fiction.

More insidiously, this kind of reading involves what the preceding chapters imply are gender-coded assumptions about the representation of "woman" in fictional discourse and the representation of female authorship in critical discourse. Like many of the established readings of Jean Rhys's novels, it seeks to account for the rejection and humiliation of a protagonist by blaming her. Like many of the early readings of *The Golden Notebook*, it tries to naturalize "unrealistic," discrepant, or conflicting aspects of the discourse by declaring them "unreal" within the fictional context, conscious or unconscious projections of the protagonist's psyche. And like several influential readings of *The Color Purple*, it is inclined to view anomalies of plotting, in particular the anticlimactic conclusion, as flaws, indicators that in writing "a book that was all tangents" (as Atwood herself described *Lady Oracle*),[3] the author was exceeding the boundaries of her own competence, which was far better displayed in the pared-down mastery of her preceding novel, *Surfacing* (1972).

But the view of Joan, and of Atwood, that this interpretation proposes is far too congruent with the dominant construction of "woman" within Western culture, in that woman's essential otherness is conventionally manifested in her culpability, her extravagance, and her need of constant control. If in many respects *Lady Oracle* actively invites the reductive reading sketched out here, it does so in a context that makes *reduction* a particularly problematic concern for women. Most obviously, this is a book in which fat is

[3]Interview with Atwood, quoted in Jerome H. Rosenberg, *Margaret Atwood* (Boston: Twayne World Authors Series, Canadian Literature, 1984), p. 112.

a feminist issue, and in which excess of body becomes symbolic of female resistance to a society that wishes to constrict women to dimensions it deems appropriate, using devices that range from exemplars to definitions to diets. More generally, this is a book in which the activity of marking limits and designating "sides" is at once a social imperative and an ontological impossibility. Despite a pervasive rhetoric of self-help, in which control and containment are the approved outward and visible signs of a valorized "secure" identity, the fictional universe of *Lady Oracle* is one in which things do not always stay in their places. In particular, boundaries between self and other and between reality and unreality can shift or even dissolve without warning.

I

The two "sides" occupying the most space in *Lady Oracle* are the universe of the "costume Gothics" that Joan writes under the pseudonym of her late, beloved Aunt Louisa K. Delacourt and the adjacent universe of the contemporary "reality" that Joan inhabits along with such characters as her mother and father, Miss Flegg of the dancing school, the malevolent Brownies, the teenage vamps who grow up to become the implied readers of her "costume Gothics," the Canadian nationalists who want to blow up the Peace Bridge, the Polish Count, the Royal Porcupine, the poet and blackmailer Fraser Buchanan, and of course her husband, Arthur. The second catalogue suggests that despite Joan's assertions to the contrary, "reality" in this novel is no more "gray and multi-dimensional and complicated" (p. 300) than the world occupied by Charlotte, Felicia, and Redmond of the imbedded romance *Stalked by Love* or, for that matter, than the world occupied by the Lady who in the imbedded poem, "Lady Oracle," *"floats down the river / singing her last song"* in free-verse imitation of Tennyson's Lady of Shalott (p. 252). Joan herself is concerned to separate her own life from the garish and violent plots that engage her heroines, but the (highly conventional) distinction she wants to invoke between art and life never quite applies to the situation at hand. For instance, reflecting on the demands of her married female friends, she decides that her own double role as public drudge and closet fantasist is a more practical solution to the problem of female heterosexual desire:

> They wanted their men to be strong, lustful, passionate and exciting, with hard rapacious mouths, but also tender and worshipful. They wanted men in mysterious cloaks who would rescue them from balconies, but they also wanted meaningful in-depth relationships and total openness. (The Scarlet Pimpernel, I would tell them silently, does not have time for meaningful, in-depth relationships.) They wanted multiple orgasms, they wanted the earth to move, but they also wanted help with the dishes. [p. 241]

The men with "hard rapacious mouths" and the men who offer "meaningful in-depth relationships" are clearly products of very different discursive codes. Precisely because the codes are so recognizable *as* codes, however, the designations "art" and "life" are inadequate to characterize them. Both kinds of men are familiar constructs, which is to say that both belong to the domain of art, or at least of artifice. Both occur in mass-market publications, albeit publications with very different controlling premises, and both kinds of publication presume the same general reading public: middle-to-working-class dissatisfied women.[4] Atwood juxtaposes the banalities of popular psychology and of self-help guides ("total openness," "help with the dishes") with the banalities of popular romance ("mysterious cloaks," "they wanted the earth to move"), thereby pointing up the socially constructed and manipulative nature of both genres. By implication, it is not "reality" that dictates a radical split between female eroticism and daily life, but the whole of a consumer culture that relegates women's sexual desire to the domain of the fantastic and so curtails "woman" as she is "realistically" represented.

In this way the primary distinction, to which Joan periodically reverts, between the "side" of the real world and the "side" of the fictional or fantastic world, is made problematic by the derivative nature of *all* Joan's experience. *Lady Oracle* is a highly satirical novel,

---

[4]Two recent and (largely) sympathetic studies of popular fiction for women and its implied and real readers are Tania Modleski, *Loving with a Vengeance: Mass-Produced Fantasies for Women* (New York: Methuen, 1982); and Janice A. Radway, *Reading the Romance: Women, Patriarchy, and Popular Literature* (Chapel Hill: University of North Carolina Press, 1984).

and the satire results not from an invasion of the real by the conventions of the artificial but from the clash of conventions belonging to different discursive practices. If incursions of rhetoric from Gothic novels or Italian *fotoromanzas* or cautionary-tale structures from such fairy stories as "The Little Mermaid" and "Bluebeard" or from such movies as *The Red Shoes* seem to signal that a passage is informed by Joan's fantasies, inasmuch as these cues reveal her psychic indebtedness to the formative fictions Western culture has produced for women, the conventions by which she is presented to the reader are similarly drawn from familiar models and similarly imbued with ideological presuppositions. *Lady Oracle* is not a novel in which the costume Gothic stands in clear opposition to the naked truth. In the imbricated worlds of this story, both clothing and nudity are acknowledged to be already coded within a number of different sign systems.

In similar ways, conventions governing appearances of the supernatural in the Gothic seep into the "real" world of Toronto and environs, with generally unsettling effects. Indeed, in many ways the function of the supernatural in *Lady Oracle* is the reverse of the function of the supernatural in the traditional Gothic, where occurrences that throughout the story appeared inexplicable from the point of view of contemporary science turn out at the conclusion to have mundane and, as a consequence, deflating explanations. For example, in the great Gothic prototype Ann Radcliffe's *Mysteries of Udolpho*, the central monitory figure, the apparent ghost of a woman who died because of her sexual transgressions, turns out to be a living woman whose "haunting" of the castle is a consequence of her insanity.[5] Claire Kahane sees in such veiled but curiously central female figures, who seem at the emotional core of all Gothics, "the spectral presence of a dead-undead mother, archaic and encompassing, a ghost signifying the problematics of femininity which the heroine must confront."[6] The conventional Gothic conclusion thus naturalizes the supernatural and renders the archaic mother harmless because illusory, unambiguously Other and thus no longer a

[5] Ann Radcliffe, *The Mysteries of Udolpho* (Oxford: Oxford University Press, 1966).
[6] Claire Kahane, "The Gothic Mirror," in *The (M)other Tongue: Essays in Feminist Psychoanalytic Interpretation*, ed. Shirley Nelson Garner, Claire Kahane, and Madelon Sprengnether (Ithaca: Cornell University Press, 1985), p. 336.

threat to established boundaries, no longer an uncanny mirror re-flecting self as other and making other eerily recognizable as self.

Kahane's feminist psychoanalytic reading of Gothic conventions clearly has applications to the self/(m)other drama in *Lady Oracle*, in particular because it suggests that individuation can never be an unproblematic concept for women. If the male child can use the fact of his sex to declare his fundamental difference from the mother who was initially his point of contact with the world, "the female child, who shares the female body and its symbolic place in our culture, remains locked in a more tenuous and fundamentally am-biguous struggle for a separate identity."[7] For a female child, to separate from the mother is to renounce what may be the only possible source of female power, a power at once more threatening and more seductive because it involves notions of merging and ob-literation, effacement of the limits with which patriarchal culture constructs and maintains its world. And as Kahane points out, the Gothic heroine gains her separate self only to lose it in a concluding heterosexual marriage. The supernatural yields to the natural; the mother yields to the husband; the Gothic protagonist has flirted with sexuality and power only to be safely reinscribed in the romance plot. Kahane summarizes her experience in reading *Udolpho*:

> Thus the novel allows me first to enjoy and then to repress the sexual and aggressive center of Udolpho, which, as the mad nun has warned, leads to madness and death, and leaves me safely enclosed—but, significantly, socially secluded—in an idealized nurturing space, the space provided for heroines by patriarchal narrative convention.[8]

Atwood is of course well aware of the founding presuppositions of the Gothic. Her projected doctoral dissertation at Harvard, which was to be titled "The English Metaphysical Romance," was to con-centrate particularly on defining structural aspects of the genre, and her remarks during interviews affirm that she was one of the earliest researchers to see the importance of the Gothic as a preeminently female form.[9] *Lady Oracle* is preoccupied both with the Gothic and

[7]Ibid., p. 337.
[8]Ibid., p. 340.
[9]Davey, *Margaret Atwood*, p. 12. Atwood speaks extensively about Gothics in Cath-rine Martens, "Mother-Figures in *Surfacing* and *Lady Oracle*: An Interview with Mar-garet Atwood," *American Studies in Scandinavia* 16 (1984), 45-54.

with the female body, a conjunction of concerns suggesting a "sexual and aggressive center" that will be treated more self-consciously, perhaps even inscribed in an altogether different register in this novel.

The supernatural events in *Lady Oracle* invariably take the form of appearances of a female body. This body is always aligned with the maternal, most obviously in the case of Joan's own mother, who makes her spectral appearances costumed in the period garments of the feminine mystique that entrapped her. In her first manifestation she is seen not by Joan but by the self-styled medium Leda Sprott, who runs the Jordan Chapel and who describes the woman standing behind Joan's chair as "about thirty, with dark hair, wearing a navy-blue suit with a white collar and a pair of white gloves" (p. 120). In the context of the seedy service that Joan is attending for the first time, this appearance seems part of the ongoing complicity between Leda Sprott and her elderly, scatty congregation—except, of course, that as Joan observes, there is no reasonable explanation for the fact that Leda Sprott knows what her mother looks like. When pressed with the information that this ghost has "broken the rules," Leda offers the hypothesis of an "astral body," which "could float around by itself, attached to you by something like a long rubber band" (p. 121), an explanation that does nothing to make the phenomenon more immediately credible but that remains uncontested throughout the narrative (except by Joan's initial "That's crazy") for lack of a more plausible theory.

This particular manifestation of Joan's mother recurs two more times in the course of Joan's narration. In the first, Joan returns to the London apartment of her new lover Arthur and his two roommates to discover her mother standing there, dressed in her 1949 navy blue suit, hat and gloves, wearing her 1949 Joan Crawford makeup, and "crying, soundlessly, horribly; mascara was running from her eyes in black tears." Despite the accumulation of detail, there is no question of this woman's being physically present in the London flat: "Through her back I could see the dilapidated sofa; it looked as though the stuffing was coming out of her" (p. 194). Five days later, Joan receives the telegram announcing her mother's death and realizes "she'd turned up in my front parlor to tell me about it" (p. 196). The last time this mother appears, she wears the same clothing and makeup and is crying the same mascaraed tears, but this time her behavior suggests a mother-daughter role reversal as well as alluding to the frame tale of another formative Gothic, *Wuthering Heights*:[10]

> She was crying soundlessly, she pressed her face against the glass like a child, mascara ran from her eyes in black tears.
> "What do you want?" I said, but she didn't answer. She stretched out her arms to me, she wanted me to come with her; she wanted us together. [p. 362]

Here the spectral mother almost lures Joan off her balcony ("She'd come very close that time, she'd almost done it," Joan reports [p. 363]), and the incident provokes the recognition "I would never be able to make her happy. . . . Maybe it was time for me to stop trying" (p. 363). Clearly the manifestations of the mother's "astral body" represent occasions for Joan to confront the complexity of her relationship to her mother and to separate herself from the impossible task of making her happy.

But confrontation and separation do not serve to naturalize these manifestations. The mother's repeated incursions into the banal "reality" inhabited by Joan remain supernatural, despite their therapeutic function. They cannot be explained, for instance, as fantasies generated by Joan's obsession with pleasing her mother: the first "astral" appearance is witnessed not by Joan but by Leda Sprott, and the second occurs before Joan has any notion that her mother has died. These semiparodic, semiserious visitations remain detached from any sort of explanatory structure that would integrate them into a coherent, fundamentally realist fictional universe. They are indicative of a tendency on the part of the female body in this novel to turn up unexpectedly and inexplicably, to transgress the limits that have been set for it, to refuse to stay in its place.

Another important manifestation of this tendency is the Fat Lady, who is at first, at least apparently, an imaginative construct based on the memory of too much flesh, which haunts Joan as a sort of

---

[10]The occasion for Lockwood's hearing the story of Cathy and Heathcliff from Nellie Dean is the spectral appearance of the child Cathy outside Lockwood's window crying, "Let me in—let me in!" Emily Brontë, *Wuthering Heights* (New York: Macmillan, 1929), p. 24.

ghostly residue of her overweight childhood. The effect of losing a hundred pounds after reaching physical maturity was to make Joan sexually desirable for the first time, while simultaneously stripping her of the enveloping flesh that had symbolized her resistance to the societal norms her mother was trying to impose and that had served, albeit ironically, as a source of power. Reminiscing about the way her size had buffered her from "the usual female fears," Joan observes that to molest her would have been "like molesting a giant basketball," and adds, "Though I treasured images of myself exuding melting femininity and soft surrender, I knew I would be able to squash any potential molestor against a wall merely by breathing out" (pp. 155–56). The process of reducing began to expose her to sexual depredations: "Strange men, whose gaze had previously slid over and around me as though I wasn't there, began to look at me from truck-cab windows and construction sites; a speculative look, like a dog eyeing a fire hydrant" (p. 135). Atwood's representation of the consequences attendant on a dramatic change in body size reveals graphically that for a woman in Western society, to be perceived as sexual is to be a potential victim.

Joan comes to realize that her fat had provided a "magic cloak of blubber and invisibility" (p. 157), which had not only protected her from unwelcome advances but had allowed her to observe the social world of her age group and to arrive at some acute insights about the women who would make up her reading public. On the other hand, this peculiar invulnerability was also construed as asexuality. "Though immersed in flesh, I was regarded as being above its desires, which of course was not true" (p. 102), she reports, marking in passing one of the most characteristic features of femininity as it is currently constructed—a tenet at the heart of such cultural myths as the story of the Little Mermaid or the film *The Red Shoes* and one of the precepts subjected to the closest scrutiny in this novel. This tenet prescribes amputation as the defining feature of female existence: getting one thing always involves giving up another. As Joan summarizes the rule, "In order to get a soul you had to suffer, and you had to give something up; or was that to get legs and feet? I couldn't remember. She'd become a dancer, though with no tongue. Then there was Moira Shearer, in *The Red Shoes*. Neither of them had been able to please the handsome prince; both of them had died" (p. 241).This formulation points up how whimsical the imperative is to choose between such evidently compatible desires as artistic creation and heterosexual love. As the plot nears its climax, however, Joan realizes that she has not been able to evade the prescription after all, and the bifurcation is revealed as not only arbitrary but damaging: "You could dance, or you could have the love of a good man. But you were afraid to dance, because you had this unnatural fear that if you danced they'd cut your feet off so you wouldn't be able to dance. Finally you overcame your fear and danced, and they cut your feet off. The good man went away too, because you wanted to dance" (p. 368).

The image of the Fat Lady that she concocts seems a response to the discovery that society requires women to be maimed to be acceptable and that even a maimed woman may not be sanctioned if her desires are considered too disruptive. The Fat Lady, as Joan conceives her, is the embodiment—literally—of the female potential for excess, of the threat that unmutilated, unchecked femininity will overflow boundaries, obliterating distinctions and violating proprieties. Significantly, she is a circus freak, a spectacle, "something that had to be seen to be believed" but that Joan is not allowed to view. Even more significant, she arises from Joan's conflation of two forbidden sideshow attractions, one featuring the traditional Fat Lady and a second featuring dancing girls in gauze pants and maroon satin brassieres (p. 97). Not only is this Fat Lady surpassingly large—Joan imagines her "fatter than the crude picture of her painted on the hoarding, much fatter than me" (p. 111)—but she is also one of her culture's avatars of active yet sexually desirable femininity, a dancer who in her second appearance wears the tiara and the pink ballerina's tutu that Joan craved as a child. Joan finds her own fantasy inappropriate, inasmuch as it seems to defy the popular platitudes about "accepting oneself" that she imagines issuing from Arthur:

> What a shame, he'd say, how destructive to me were the attitudes of society, forcing me into a mold of femininity that I could never fit, stuffing me into those ridiculous pink tights, those spangles, those outmoded, cramping ballet slippers. How much better for me if I'd been

> accepted for what I was and had learned to accept myself, too. Very
> true, very right, very pious. But it's still not so simple. I wanted those
> things, that fluffy skirt, that glittering tiara. I liked them. [p. 112]

Paradoxically, these pieties about self-acceptance only confirm that
Joan herself is not acceptable, precisely because she wants too much.
Her "self" exceeds the requisite ideological containers.

As the plot develops, the Fat Lady becomes excessive in other
respects, intruding herself into the action in ways that are less and
less reconcilable with the premise that she is Joan's fantasy. As if
she has irremediably forgotten her place, she finally emerges un-
heralded and unanticipated in the middle of that Canadian national
ritual of male bonding, a hockey game, which Arthur is watching
on television: "The Fat Lady skated out onto the ice. I couldn't help
myself. It was one of the most important moments of my life, I
should have been able to keep her away, but out she came in a pink
skating costume, her head ornamented with swan's-down" (p. 304).
At this point, when Joan is contemplating the necessity of telling
Arthur about one of her "other" lives, the Fat Lady figures simultaneously as a sign of Joan's lack of self-control and as a character
who has become autonomous to the point where she herself is violating both social and textual prohibitions. As Joan watches, the
Fat Lady floats to the top of the screen like a helium balloon and
remains there.

> The U.S. team scooted across the bottom of the screen like a centipede,
> but no one paid any attention, they were all distracted by the huge
> pink balloon that bobbed with such poor taste above their heads. . . .
> The Fat Lady kicked her skates feebly; her tights and the huge moon
> of her rump were visible. Really it was an outrage. "They've gone for
> the harpoon gun," I heard the commentator say. They were going to
> shoot her down in cold blood, explode her, despite the fact that she
> had now burst into song. . . . [pp. 305]

Like all the Fat Lady episodes, this passage incorporates important
elements of Joan's previous experience: the "huge moon of her
rump" offering a target to the harpoon gun recalls the conjunction
of events involving Aunt Lou's mysterious death and Joan's wound-
ing by a prankster's arrow; "she had now burst into song" brings
together a complex of allusions to singing, which figures in this

novel both as an expression of agony and as a paradigm of art,[11] and here is explicitly aligned with death (albeit in a fairly ludicrous context) because of its association with the Disney cartoon *The Whale Who Wanted to Sing at the Met.* But this implicitly climactic manifestation of the Fat Lady makes an incision within the "reality" of Joan's fictional universe. Whereas the Fat Lady was previously identified as a fantasy, she has now gone beyond Joan's management to the point where such apparent inhabitants of the gray and multi-dimensional world as the television commentator are so distracted by her extravagant otherness that they are attempting to destroy her. Yet this scene can also be read as the production of Joan's involuntary imagination, as a full-scale hallucination, for Arthur continues to watch stolidly, his gaze relegating this exorbitant Other and all the confusion she generates to the side of the unreal.

Arthur's gaze here acts as agent of the naturalizing impetus within the narrative, denying visibility to the spectacular by assigning it a psychic and indeed a pathological origin. Not coincidentally, naturalization of this sort is always a male move in *Lady Oracle,* while the tendency to see something instead of nothing is female. The body of the Fat Lady, like the "astral body" of Joan's mother, is a figure for the other "selves" that Joan—and other women as well—inhabit because the social definition of "woman" is too constricted to accommodate them. Such bodies are also surplus that the realist narrative cannot accommodate, representations of "woman" that exceed the patriarchal gesture whereby the real is defined and contained. Like the Fat Lady at the hockey game, they bob disconcertingly above the "real" action, distracting attention despite the masculinist insistence that there is "really" *nothing to be seen.*

II

Lady Oracle is concerned with how the female body, as a figure for female desire, becomes both spectacular and invisible within a cul-

---

[11]One of the most poignant passages making this association occurs early in the narrative, when Joan recalls wanting to be an opera singer: "It always appealed to me: to be able to stand up there in front of everyone and shriek as loud as you could, about hatred and love and rage and despair, scream at the top of your lungs and have it come out music" (p. 83).

ture wishing to restrict the "real" to masculinist desire and its objects. The phrase *nothing to be seen* is particularly resonant in this context of curtailing or dismissing the female body because of its centrality in Freud's account of the castration complex. According to Freud, this complex arises from the little boy's (and, symmetrically, the little girl's) discovery that the mother does not have a penis. But the assumption that the absence of a penis leaves "nothing" visible seems already implicated in an ideology in which only some "things" count as existents. As Luce Irigary observes in her monumental critique of the Western philosophical tradition, *Speculum of the Other Woman*, Freud's translation of "no penis" into "no thing" amounts to a leap into the universal that is paradigmatic of a discourse founding itself on the unicity and centrality of the phallus. "*Nothing to be seen is equivalent to having no thing,*" Irigaray writes. "*No being and no truth.*"[12] That is, the *judgment* "nothing to be seen," imposing as it does the primacy of the visible, the unitary, the monolithic embodied in the phallus *as* sex—as the only possible sex organ and therefore as the only possible mark of sexual identity—establishes woman in this discourse as possessor of no-thing; and thus as non-sex, as non-being, as deficiency, as object against which the subject asserts himself and into which, conveniently, he inserts himself.[13]

It is important to note that the discourse in which this judgment, *nothing to be seen*, finds its place is not limited to psychoanalysis. If Irigaray begins *Speculum of the Other Woman* with a reading of Freud on feminine sexuality, she does so because she finds his writing particularly illustrative of the ways in which difference is absorbed into what she terms the economy of the Same, the entirety of the dominant culture, inasmuch as this culture constructs Others by excluding them. One of her more violent formulations, "*The slit is sewn up,*" illustrates how more-than-one-thing—the labia of the vagina, to cite her most famous example—must be forcibly reduced to no-thing if this economy is to function.

[12]Luce Irigaray, *Speculum of the Other Woman* (Ithaca: Cornell University Press, 1985), p. 48.
[13]Jane Gallop points out that centering sexuality exclusively on the phallus points up the constructed nature of *masculine* sexuality as well. See her essay "*Quand Nos Lèvres S'Ecrivent*: Irigaray's Body Politic," *Romanic Review* 74, no. 1 (1983), 78–79.

The more general issue for Irigaray is the philosophical problem called the One and the Many, and the discourse in question in *Speculum* is, rather alarmingly, the entirety of Western intellectual history. Irigaray goes on to suggest in her readings of Plato, Aristotle, Descartes, Kant, Hegel, and perhaps most insidiously, in the excerpt from Plotinus's *Enneads*, which is quoted without comment, that the "problem" of the One and the Many in this tradition has traditionally been the problem of getting the Many subsumed under the One before they cause any trouble, preferably as some version of No-Thing into which the One can comfortably fit itself. Female genitals, and indeed the polymorphous character of female sexual experience,[14] become in this discussion a site of difference, an insinuation of otherness figured most subversively as the "other woman" wedged into the interstices of an apparently monolithic discourse. The problem of writing *about* difference, specifically about female sexual pleasure, here becomes emblematic of the problem of writing difference, writing differently, outside of or alongside of or in the gaps within the dominant discourse. Irigaray asks how the woman of Freud's master narrative is to find "symbols for the state of 'this nothing to be seen,' to defend its goals, or to lay claim to its rewards. *Here again no economy would be possible whereby sexual reality can be represented by/for women.*"[15] Yet the impossibility is precisely a function of a masculinist "economy" defined (by its upholders) as completely coherent, subject to no dispersal, no irreconcilable differences between the systems—or stories—that compose it. Later she asks, "But what if the 'object' started to speak? . . . What disaggregation of the subject would that entail?"[16] The question has provoked enormous controversy because it seems to imply contradictory activities: giving voice to silence, articulating the formless void that is no-thing.

A number of theorists have accordingly concluded, given this account of the operation by which the dominant culture constitutes "woman" as so radically Other that her difference amounts to non-

---

[14]According to Gallop, "the multiplicity of female genitals [is] a textual production" and not a biological "fact," but Irigaray's writing uses this production to create a "referential illusion" of polyvocality that has "a surprising, vulgar political efficacy" (pp. 79–80).

[15]Irigaray, *Speculum*, p. 49 (Irigaray's italics).

[16]Ibid., p. 135.

existence, that asking "woman" to *speak* entails a logical impossibility. Shoshana Felman states the problem succinctly: "If 'the
woman' is precisely the Other of any conceivable Western theoretical
locus of speech, how can the woman as such be speaking in this
book?"[17] Of course, Felman's formulation "any *conceivable* Western
theoretical locus of speech" is hyperbolic, in that Irigaray's project
is precisely to *conceive* other-wise; and to note the hyperbole is to
point up the answer to a question that is not, after all, merely rhetorical. In Irigaray's writing, the economy of the Same is not monolithic; the codes or narratives making up Western culture are not
joined seamlessly, and as a consequence, what is outside is not
always unambiguously dismissable as silence or no-thing. There is
always the possibility of speaking through the gaps, of exploiting
the contradictions within a system that cannot afford to acknowledge
its own self-division.

Irigaray's own gestures and especially her own practice in *Speculum* and such later productions as "When Our Lips Speak Together" suggest how the ostensible "silence" to which "woman" is
relegated might turn into a voice. If there can be no clearly delineated
Other language, no direct route to the articulation of difference, it
follows that difference must use the language of the Same—if rather
differently. That is, representation must be skewed or oblique, a
perverse mimesis employing the sort of concave mirror that is the
primary image of the speculum for Irigaray, the mirror that inverts
the image as a condition of reflecting it. Mimesis as mimicry; representation with a difference. The method of *Speculum of the Other
Women* suggests that one means to this end is a miming of the
phallocentric discourse of the dominant culture and that through
emphasis and through pursuit of implications to a reductio ad ab-
surdum such a miming can allow readers to glimpse the motivating
force that keeps this discourse entire and returning on itself. A
second means to this end might well be a miming of the feminine
as deficiency, as an otherness claimed to be the necessary supple-

[17]Shoshana Felman, "The Critical Phallacy," *Diacritics* 5 (Winter 1975), 2–10. Barbara Godard also raises this point with respect to *Lady Oracle* in a brilliant and significantly nonreductive essay, "My (M)other, My Self: Strategies for Subversion in
Atwood and Hébert," *Essays on Canadian Writing* 26 (Summer 1983), 13–44. See also
Roslyn Belkin, "The Worth of the Shadow: Margaret Atwood's *Lady Oracle*," *Thalia*
1, no. 3 (1979), 3–8.

ment to masculine sufficiency. By and large, this is the method of Freud's celebrated hysterics. Irigaray's analysis indicates that it may be the method of "other women" as well.

For the question about whether it is possible to *write* difference ought to lead irresistibly to a second, more pragmatic question: if difference were written, could anyone *see* it? This whole book begins from the premises that there are women writers who perceive the discourse into which they are, willy-nilly, inscribed as radically gendered; who have perceived themselves as in some respects ill fitted for or poorly inserted into the economy of the Same; who have attempted to write about sexual difference from and within this economy; and who in the process have attempted to adapt the language to their own uses—to write differently. For all the authors under consideration here, writing difference has involved a degree of mimicry that becomes politically significant inasmuch as it diverges from its purported models, becomes representation with a twist. The example of *Lady Oracle* raises the question in its most problematic form because in the narrative voice of this novel Atwood deliberately apes the culturally constructed "feminine," an activity that Sandra Gilbert has termed "female female impersonation."[18]

For example, in the opening of the novel, Joan is engaged in the anomalous enterprise of narrating in the past tense the events leading up to her own death:

> I planned my death carefully; unlike my life, which meandered along from one thing to another, despite my feeble efforts to control it. My life had a tendency to spread, to get flabby, to scroll and festoon like the frame of a baroque mirror, which came from following the line of least resistance. I wanted my death, by contrast, to be neat and simple, understated, even a little severe, like a Quaker church or the basic black dress with a single strand of pearls much praised by fashion magazines when I was fifteen. [p. 3]

---

[18]Sandra Gilbert, "Female Female Impersonators: The Sardonic Heroinism of Edna St.-Vincent Millay and Marianne Moore" (lecture, Cornell University, 23 March 1986). Mary Russo glosses, "If hysteria is understood as feminine in its image, accoutrements, and stage business (rather than in its physiology), then it may be used to rig us up (for lack of the phallic term) into discourse" ("Female Grotesques: Carnival and Theory," in *Feminist Studies: Critical Studies* [Bloomington: Indiana University Press, 1986], p. 223).

But any sense that the situation of posthumous narration presents a genuine mystery requiring serious elucidation is immediately countered by the voice of the narrator. In fact, this narrator is so recognizable and so conventional in function that her very presence at first seems sufficient to deflate and neutralize serious questioning. She belongs in the tradition of Lucille Ball or Gracie Allen, or in the realm of authorial personae, someone like Jean Kerr or Erma Bombeck. Her characteristic tone is rueful but fatalistic—silly me, I always mess up—for this is that great comic figure the castrated woman, woman as wholly and ludicrously other, woman with—and as— *nothing to be seen*. Yet the construction of reality that renders her invisible also requires her to be a spectacle—as she must be in order to reenact the endless drama of her identity, in which she comes up yet another time against the recognition of her own nature as deficiency or lack—specifically as deficiency or lack *of control*. Here, very clearly, what is missing is a principle of containment, something that will keep the speaker in one piece. In this opening passage, Joan has announced her failure of integrity in the root sense: she is for some curious reason unable to stay together.

Her retrospective narration goes on to chronicle how she grew up by multiplying into separate "selves," beginning from the experience of becoming "a different person" after her weight loss, a process of acquiring "the right shape" that involved discovering she now had "the wrong past" (p. 157). She discovered that this dwindling into femininity required her to diminish herself further by choosing an already-established role, an act that required amputating not only "the wrong past" but great portions of the present as well. In dealing with Arthur's roommates, for example, she learned, "One could not, apparently, be both a respected female savant and a scullery maid" (p. 190), and fearing that her "costume Gothics" made her intellectually unrespectable in Arthur's eyes, she in effect chose the scullery maid role in his presence, playing the devoted if inept wife and turning out the pages only when he wasn't looking. The seductions of the Gothic in turn led her to locate a third "self," whose unconscious existence at the heart of the self/(m)other labyrinth became the impetus for still another kind of secret—albeit stereotypically "feminine"—writing. This figure came into being as Joan pieced together words she had written during passages of self-hypnosis. Joan enters the subterranean region of this "lady oracle" through a mirror, itself a duplicate of the three-sided dressing table mirror of her childhood that revealed her mother as hydra-headed, uncontrolled, "a monster" (p. 70). The device of the mirror as entry suggests that the powerful, unhappy, somehow maternal persona of the poem is the reverse or repressed side of the "happy and inept" persona (p. 248) that Joan allows herself and is allowed by the society represented most powerfully by her husband, the self-styled political radical whose entire mode of functioning presumes her continued presence as a "nourishing blob" (p. 236).

Yet the narrative voice presents this socially mandated dis-integration largely as a failure of self-containment, one that implies other breaches of integrity, to which Joan will also admit, ruefully. For instance, she confesses to being chronically dishonest, at first unwilling to tell the truth because of her perception of the probable consequences—"In my experience, honesty and expressing your feelings could lead to only one thing. Disaster" (p. 37)—but later, and worse, unable even to identify "the truth" among so many plausible contenders. Reporting on the Polish Count's accusation that she had a lover, she confides ingenuously, "I'd always found other people's versions of reality very influential and I was beginning to think that maybe he was right, maybe I did have a secret lover" (p. 180). Here, as elsewhere in the narrative, "other people's versions of reality" are more conventional and more coherent than her own, and the demands that *she* be conventional and coherent tend to act as regulatory principles prompting her to condemn her own story for its exuberance. But she also draws from the experience the correct lesson: the problem is not that she tells lies, but that her lies are not in accordance with current norms of realism, not in the most ordinary sense credible. As she admits, "I told lies but they were not water-tight. My mind was not disciplined, as Arthur sometimes pointed out" (p. 170). Indeed, she interprets all her imaginative produc-tions—lies, fantasies, dreams, hypnotic journeys, poetry and "cos-tume Gothics"—as evidence of an essential *lack*, an absence that manifests itself as a plenitude, a superabundance of things that must be continually reconstrued as no-thing.

By her own account, then, the deficiency to which Joan so cheer-fully admits resides in her excessiveness. Excess as deficiency is a paradox, of course, but it is a paradox familiar to any woman who has been schooled in the rigorous requirements of femininity. To take one example, the basic black dress with the single strand of pearls invoked at the opening of the novel is a classic emblem of feminine restraint that is also a class marker. The women who are the most valuable commodities in Joan's society are got up in this reticent style, whereas less costly women tend to be tricked out in the spangles and gaudy colors that Joan herself favors. The heroines of the mass-market novels that she writes (the name "costume Goth-ics" reflects her strong sense of the priority of clothing in the sign system in which where she herself is inscribed) also favor restraint, as opposed to the counterpoised bad women, whose badness is figured precisely in the fact that they, like Joan, cannot contain themselves. The two opposed female characters in her costume-Gothic-in-progress *Stalked by Love* illustrate her mastery of the mas-culinist code whereby containment of the feminine translates into (among other things) sexual desirability:

> *He was thinking of Charlotte. He liked making her blush. He'd become tired of the extravagance of Felicia: of her figure that spread like crabgrass, her hair that spread like fire, her mind that spread like cancer or pubic lice. "Contain your-self," he'd said to her, more than once, but she couldn't contain herself, she raged over him like a plague, leaving him withered. But Charlotte now, with her stays and her peculiar ways, her white flannelette face, her bleached fingers . . . her coolness intrigued him.* [p.351]

Not surprisingly, the rampant Felicia looks a great deal like Joan, who manipulates the formulaic phrases of her genre in a fairly un-controlled way herself, touch-typing with her eyes closed and so mimicking a prevailing ideology. But her own mastery of the for-mulas continually reminds her that she is not living up to expectations.

Her whole history, of course, is one of not living up to expectations by dint of being far *more* than what is required, even though she generally exceeds demands precisely because of her desire to please. For instance, the poem resulting from her experiments with auto-matic writing, "Lady Oracle," is described by variously enthusiastic and appalled male characters as "a cross between Kahlil Gibran and Rod McKuen" (pp. 250, 265), and the account of its reception sug-gests that in her possession of a truly mass-market unconscious Joan has once again became too much of a good thing, ultimately monstrous in her naive ability to outdo her ostensible creators, the press agents and publicists who cater to public appetites. All such excesses are presented as displacements of the excess of body that characterized Joan as a child. As a child, she ate not only to triumph over a mother who quite literally embodied the societal norm but also in an attempt to translate herself out of the realm of contingency, to guarantee her existence by overflowing assigned boundaries to become "solid, solid as a stone so she wouldn't be able to get rid of me" (pp. 82–83).[19] This excessive body never really leaves her, despite a precipitate weight loss; or rather, she does not lose her boundless body so much as gain a plurality of bodies, chief among them the spectral mother and the Fat Lady. These bodies function as weirdly corporeal alter egos, haunting her when she tries to confine herself to a single slender identity.

The discussion in the previous section has suggested some of the ways in which these bodies progressively elude her control, finally escaping beyond the naturalizing powers of the realist narrative. In a similar manner, aspects of the ostensibly "controlling" plot are infiltrated by apparently discordant elements of the Gothic in ways that cannot be explained simply by a tendency on the part of the narrator to see the "real" world through Gothic lenses. The most important instances occur near the end of the narrative, when Joan, who is becoming increasingly anxious because of the pressure of keeping her three identities separate, breaks off her relationship with the Royal Porcupine and begins to receive heavy-breathing telephone calls and to find dead animals with threatening messages attached to them lying on her doorstep. At first she attributes these memento mori to her rejected lover, who after all has to his credit an exhibition of frozen road kills. Then she suspects her erstwhile blackmailer Fraser Buchanan. But both men are convincing in their denials, and neither has any obvious reason for menacing her in this way. Mulling over the clues, she considers, "Perhaps one person

---

[19]In *Lady Oracle*, Atwood offers one of the first feminist analyses of obesity as an implicitly political response to social demands on women. Kim Chernin builds on this analysis in *The Obsession: Reflections on the Tyranny of Slenderness* (New York: Harper Colophon Books, 1981). See also Susie Orbach's landmark work on female body image, *Fat Is a Feminist Issue* (New York: Berkley, 1978).

was doing the animals, another the notes, a third the phone calls ... but I couldn't believe that. It had to be a single person, with a plan, a plot that had some end in view" (p. 325). The hypothesis of a single agent and a single plot is rooted in literary conventions, of course, but these particular conventions privilege restraint and compactness, values associated with the "real" word of the novel, as opposed to the dilation and extravagance that are offered as Joan's besetting sins and symptoms of the feminine waywardness that causes the story to "scroll and festoon" away from linearity and closure.[20] If Joan's solution to the mystery relies on Gothic precedent, it is also economical: "Then all at once I knew. It was Arthur. The whole thing was Arthur. He'd found out about the Royal Porcupine, he must've known for some time. He'd been watching me all along, not saying anything; it would be like him not to say anything. But he'd made a decision about me finally, a pronouncement, thumbs down, I was unworthy, I would have to go, and this was his plan to get rid of me" (p. 325).

The reasoning makes perfect sense given the entirety of the action so far. First of all, this behavior is completely in character for the man whose only regular activity has been represented as judging and repudiating former associates. Second, only Arthur has a credible motive for threatening Joan, in that only Arthur has in any significant respect been betrayed by her multiple identities. Third, Arthur has by far the greatest opportunity both to spy on Joan and to deliver the messages when she is least likely to expect them.

Of course, the reasoning is also consistent with the "central plot" of the Gothic, which Atwood has identified as the apprehension "my husband is trying to kill me."[21] Certainly Joan, who says later that she is "hooked on plots" (p. 342), deals over and over with this apprehension as her life turns more and more Gothic. But Atwood goes on to suggest that the popularity of the Gothic may rest on reader recognition: "I think it is consumed in such great quantities by women because secretly they think their husbands are trying to

---

[20]Patricia Parker brilliantly traces the long association between the figure of the fat lady and rhetorical strategies of dilation and copiousness in "Literary Fat Ladies and the Generation of the Text," in Patricia Parker, *Literary Fat Ladies: Rhetoric, Gender, Property* (London: Methuen, 1987), pp. 8–35.

[21]Martens, "Mother-Figures," p. 49.

kill them."²² The potentiality of men to be murderers as well as rescuers of dependent women is inscribed in the culture, as well as in the fictions the culture produces. The "plot" against women, and particularly against wives, is not only, and not even primarily, something that writers of Gothics create. For this reason, it is important that the Gothic elements in *Lady Oracle* cannot be psychologized satisfactorily, even though they mesh with Joan's own psychic proclivities. The telephone calls, the dead animals, and the threatening messages are indubitably part of the landscape that Joan shares with Arthur. They are not merely her fictions, fantasies, or hallucinations. They demand an explanation in the "real" world.

Joan stages a fake drowning and leaves Canada for the Italian village of Terremoto, "moving earth." The name has affinities with the popular romance tradition ("they wanted the earth to move"), but it also suggests ontological instability: the ground on which the apparent frame story rests may well have the propensity to shift without warning. There she constructs a Gothic analogue to her own situation, sending the bad woman/wife/sacrificial victim Felicia, the character with whom she identifies in spite of the informing values of the genre, into the maze that has functioned as structural metaphor for both the generic Gothic plot and the plot of *Lady Oracle*. The climactic scene at the center of this maze begins with a passage that is strikingly similar to the recognition scene in which she deduced that Arthur was the source of the anonymous threats; then it modulates into a conflation of her own situation with Felicia's.

> *Then she knew. Redmond was the killer. He was a killer in disguise, he wanted to murder her as he had murdered his other wives. . . . Then she would always have to stay here with them, at the center of the maze. . . . He wanted to replace her with the other one, the next one, thin and flawless . . . .*
>
> *"Don't touch me," she said, taking a step backward. She refused to be doomed. As long as she stayed on her side of the door she would be safe. Cunningly, he began his transformations, trying to lure her into his reach. His face grew a white gauze mask, then a pair of mauve-tinted spectacles, then a red beard and moustache, which faded, giving place to burning eyes and icicle teeth. Then his cloak vanished and he stood looking at her sadly; he was wearing a turtle-neck sweater.*
>
> *"Arthur?" she said. Could he ever forgive her?* [p. 376–77]

²²Ibid.

The transformations undergone by the hitherto rapacious-mouthed Redmond take him through the identities of the men that have had most influence on Joan: her father, the commando and anesthetist, whom she cannot quite get over suspecting of having killed her mother; the Polish Count, Paul, who believed that women want to be raped and that in a woman physical deformity is worse than idiocy; the Royal Porcupine, Chuck Brewer, who tried first to compete with her and then to persuade her to leave Arthur for him; and the man in the ravine, who has both exposed himself to the young Joan and given her a daffodil and who has become the prototype for the enigmatic partner of the powerful, unhappy woman in the poem "Lady Oracle." In this passage, these men are evidently threatening, and their appearances here disclose the threat that has always been latent in each of them.

When Arthur emerges, however, he triggers only reflexive guilt: "*Could he ever forgive her?*" Of all the men in her story, he is the only one to have arisen from her Gothic imagination, in that Joan met him while she was acting out a scene she intended to write and in fact mistook him for the villain of her piece. Of all the men in her story, he is also the only one whom she has not presented as inherently dubious, as duplicitous, as a potential "killer in disguise." She is, in fact, fondly solicitous of the qualities she deems marks of his innocence or eccentricity—his lack of curiosity about the many university extension courses she claims to be taking in order to account for the time she spends writing, for instance, or his propensity to be aware of her existence only in the moments between the peaks of his ideological fervor and the troughs of his political disillusionment (p. 236). Their marriage, she has continually pointed out, is ordinary, normal, in fact better than average. And this representation of a "working" marriage is part of a commentary on the notion of marriage as a desired outcome, the terminus of the romance plot.

Joan's Gothic continues toward its climax:

> Redmond resumed his opera cloak. His mouth was hard and rapacious, his eyes smoldered. "Let me take you away," he whispered. "Let me rescue you. We will dance together forever, always."
>
> "Always," she said, almost yielding. "Forever." Once she had wanted these words, she had waited all her life for someone to say them. . . . She

pictured herself whirling slowly across a ballroom floor, a strong arm around
her waist. . . .
   "No," she said. "I know who you are."
   The flesh fell away from his face, revealing the skull behind it; he stepped
towards her, reaching for her throat. . . . [p. 377]

The dance that has been Joan's metaphor for the ideal merger of art
and heterosexual love has become a dance of death, symbolic of the
union that terminates the traditional Gothic and embalms its heroine
forever in the romance plot. Despite its seductive twining, this plot
is linear and teleological. It leads somewhere, and its climax reveals
its ultimate malignancy. When the heroine has negotiated the maze
and has finally reached its center to become the sanctioned object
of desire, she is so reduced by having achieved coincidence with
the demands of the hero and the society he represents that she is
in effect inanimate, "placed" forever in an attenuated identity defined and controlled wholly by the man who bestows it. More insidiously, she is now in the position of the wife, and thus the bad
woman, the victim, whom the hero must transcend in order to aspire
toward fresh objects of desire, toward "the next one, thin and flaw-
less." Always ready to identify with the wrong woman on the other
side of the story, the one who violates boundaries and refuses to
remain on one side, Joan had reflected earlier, "In a fairy tale I would
be one of the two stupid sisters who open the forbidden door and
are shocked by the murdered wives, not the third, clever one who
keeps to the essentials: presence of mind, foresight, the telling of
watertight lies" (p. 170). The story behind the story of romantic love
is the story of Bluebeard, and she knows that in this narrative tradition for every triumphant survivor there is a roomful of corpses.

   Yet at this crisis point in the novel, when Joan opens her eyes,
hears footsteps, and reports, "I opened the door. I knew who it
would be" (p. 377), Atwood averts the revelation that seems encoded
both in Gothic precedent and in the internal logic of the plot. Despite
the fact that Joan has in effect sent for Arthur and despite the evidence that Arthur is the only possible source of the threatening calls,
messages, and dead animals, the man on the other side of the door
is a complete stranger. Even more significant, in the final chapter
where this discovery is reported, the narrative voice reverts to the
chatty disorganization that is the characteristic note of the castrated

woman: "I didn't really mean to hit him with the Cinzano bottle. I mean, I meant to hit someone, but it wasn't personal. I'd never seen him before in my life, he was a complete stranger. I guess I just got carried away: he looked like someone else . . . (p. 378)." Whereas the penultimate chapter promised to reveal the mystery at the center of the labyrinth—the identity of the man trying to kill the protagonist—this final chapter returns the discourse to banality. The most extreme plot complication is never resolved. There is no further mention of the messages or the dead animals. Instead, Joan resumes responsibility for most of the events of the story: "It did make a mess; but then, I don't think I'll ever be a very tidy person" (p. 380). Her own flakiness, her psychic dispersal and lack of control, are once again presented as the key problems.

In this way, Atwood carefully betrays her implicit ending, an ending whose implications have been worked out with equal care in Joan's revision of the conclusion to her own novel, *Stalked by Love*. In the process, "stalked by love" is revealed to be an appropriate title as well as a typical one. Earlier Joan confided that she had been trying for years to get the words *love* and *terror* into the same title (p. 32), and in this final exploration of the Gothic structure it seems that the sanctioned conclusion, the "rescue" that wrenches the heroine away from the horrors and temptations of the maternal body and restores her to the patriarchy by subsuming her to the hero in marriage, exposes the most fundamental source of violence in the genre: in a society that defines all possible male-female relations in terms of masculine control and constraint, heterosexual love *is* terror for women. The intricate skein of power relations that allows the hero to "save" the heroine by claiming her as his own is far more entangling and entrapping than the feminine labyrinth.

But Atwood displays this revelation within the imbedded narrative only to withhold it from the frame narrative. As a consequence, it remains an insinuated climax that can gesture toward an unequivocal closure without in any way realizing that closure. By the logic of the plot, the point of *Lady Oracle* might well be that all men are killers, given the right circumstances. As Joan reflects when she is wondering whether her father murdered her mother, "Anything is the sort of thing anyone would do, given the right circumstances" (p. 200), and when "circumstances" consist of a version of reality that builds dominance into its fundamental structure, the privileged will inevitably be oppressors. In a subsequent novel, *Bodily Harm* (1982), Atwood gave this observation a much darker formulation: the reiterated answer to the question of why people in power—colonialists, whites, men—do unspeakable things to other people is "because they can get away with it," "because they can."[23] In *Lady Oracle*, however, she is committed to exploring the assumptions behind the question. Is the masculinist version of "reality," which builds dominance into its fundamental structure, the only version of reality? The only conceivable version? The only imaginable version? Is it pervasive, seamless, universal? Does it rule out all other possibilities? Is there no place for "woman" beyond the impossibly constricted role the masculinist culture has provided for her? And if "woman" speaks, can her voice do anything more than affirm the established asymmetries, resonate as the silence in opposition to which the masculine logos emerges as present and powerful?

It is precisely the tone of *Lady Oracle*—its familiarity, its banality, its flakiness—that precludes such a grim resolution. In her extreme dispersal, which she represents as her characteristic "untidiness," the castrated woman forestalls any such climactic recognition, and in this gesture defers forever the narrative closure that would enclose her in the romance plot. The emphasis shifts to the character and to the character's act of storytelling and away from the threatened ending of the story. The model for the narrative thus shifts abruptly to therapy: self-revelation, or talking cure. To be sure, the desired end of such a "cure" is still the restoration of the speaker to the patriarchal order, an outcome that Jacques Lacan has termed the "repatriation of alienated signifiers."[24] And in the concluding chapter of *Lady Oracle*, Atwood has Joan embracing the implications of "repatriation" with the same enthusiasm that she has brought to the recognition of her status as excessively deficient, abundantly

<hr/>

[23]Margaret Atwood, *Bodily Harm* (New York: Bantam, 1982), pp. 114, 280. Other formulations of the principle occur on pp. 134, 167, 170 and 240. *The Handmaid's Tale* (1986) is in many respects the story of *how* they can and what they do.

[24]I am indebted to Dianne Hunter's essay, "Hysteria, Psychoanalysis, and Feminism: The Case of Anna O.," in *The (M)other Tongue*, pp. 89–115, for cuing my own feminist rereading of this loaded phrase.

deprived. Eagerly admitting all her putative former errors, Joan resolves to return to Canada, her *patria*, and to submit herself to the
paternal law governing the economy of the Same, which she has
ambiguously violated by an act of perverse mirroring: she has mis-
represented her escape as her death. Furthermore, a culminating
revelation makes "repatriation" such an encompassing metaphor
that it dictates a radical reinterpretation of the entire preceding story.
Joan has not herself been the author of her own confession. In return
for immunity from prosecution, she has already turned over the
ownership of her signifiers to the phallic pen of the reporter who
had been on the Other Side of the door: "It was nice of him not to
press charges when he came to. At first I thought it was only because
he wanted the story: reporters are like that. I talked too much, of
course, but I was feeling nervous. I guess it will make a pretty weird
story, once he's written it; and the odd thing is that I didn't tell any
lies. Well, not very many. Some of the names and a few other things,
but nothing major"(p. 378).

But the emphasis on the *triviality* of the lies, occurring as it does
in a context that affirms loquacity as one of Joan's characteristic
deficiencies, suggests that on the contrary, the entire narrative has
been mediated not only by the paternal authority of the male ghost
writer[25] but by Joan's equally characteristic tendency to fabricate
identities as a bid for male approval. The seemingly regressive move
whereby the entire narrative is recuperated as a masculinist production, a confession "as told to" a controlling masculine author,
thus establishes the whole inflated narrative as equivocally revelatory, if indeed it reveals anything at all about Joan's purported problems. In acknowledging herself to be congenitally lacking, eternally
prone to dilation and prevarication, Joan has wiggled out of the
authority for her own story. Instead, she has affirmed her identity
as "an artist, an escape artist," someone who resists enclosures
ranging from the romance plot to the universe in which all men are
potential killers: "I'd sometimes talked about love and commitment,
but the real romance of my life was that between Houdini and his

[25]Robert Lecker introduces this phrase in his analysis of the multiple narrative
voice in *Lady Oracle*—a voice that insinuates "every 'I' is a lie" (p. 194). See his "Janus
Through the Looking Glass: Atwood's First Three Novels," in *The Art of Margaret
Atwood*, ed. Davidson and Davidson, pp. 177–203.

ropes and locked trunk; entering the embrace of bondage, slithering out again. What else had I ever done?" (p. 367).

III

In this way, *Lady Oracle* presents the characteristically "feminine" deficiencies of excess, uncontrollability, and unreliability as means of evading the already-inscribed plots that act as conspiracies against woman as Other—that is, in both the Irigarayan and the Gothic sense, against the Other woman. This notion of narration as a re-tracing of well-worn paths to a preordained and patriarchically sanctioned conclusion is dramatized in Joan's first attempt at writing the climax of *Stalked by Love*, where a female character enters the Gothic labyrinth. As convention dictates, this character is the self-contained and exemplary heroine Charlotte, who reaches the center of the maze to find only *"an open gravelled oblong with a border of flowers, the daffodils already in bloom. Disappointingly, it was empty"* (p. 366). But the initial naturalization of a formerly uncanny "center" leads her on to the naturalistic solution of the whole mystery while placing her in danger so that the hero must intervene to rescue her:

> *From behind her came a mocking laugh—Felicia's! "There wasn't room for both of us," she said, "One of us had to die."*
>
> *Just as Charlotte was sinking into unconsciousness, Felicia was flung aside like a bundle of old clothes, and Charlotte was gazing up into the dark eyes of Redmond. "My darling," he breathed hoarsely. Strong arms lifted her, his warm lips pressed her own.* [p. 366]

In this first, socially sanctioned version of the Gothic climax, Charlotte's defining neatness—she is hampered from escape by her attempt to wind up her yarn as she runs—betrays her. But if this betrayal delivers her over to her enemy, it thereby makes her available to the "strong arms" of the hero, who can now intervene to rescue her, establishing himself as loving rather than menacing and establishing her as the heroine, the female character who is guaranteed survival precisely because she has been susceptible to victimization. The malignant enemy has been revealed as both natural and female, and her motive affirms the ideology that governs the romance plot: "There wasn't room for both of us. . . . One of us had to die." Just as the feminine, maternal maze in the traditional Gothic exists to be rendered unamazing, the Other woman exists to be exorcised as redundant, in the way, *too much* to be accommodated by the heterosexual couple embodying the forces of resolution and restoration in this genre.

At this point Joan expresses for the first time her dissatisfaction with her inherited plot: "That was the way it was supposed to go, that was the way it had always gone before, but somehow it no longer felt right. I'd taken a wrong turn somewhere; there was something, some fact or clue, that I had overlooked" (pp. 366–67). Her conviction that this "repatriating" resolution is inadequate to the sense of possibility generated by the preceding story suggests that "repatriation" itself is a version of the amputation principle whereby women can make gains only by making complementary sacrifices. In the Gothic, a woman gains safety and a place in society by sacrificing the power associated with the maternal body, and by the logic of the plot this sacrifice involves estranging herself from the Other woman—from the threatening possibilities of her own status as Other and from the potential power inherent in female association. Conversely, in Joan's epic poem, "Lady Oracle," the eponymous heroine is "enormously powerful, almost like a goddess," but the price she pays is as familiar a component of contemporary stories about career women as it is of fairy tales—"it was an unhappy power" (p. 248)—and the plot in which she figures inverts the Gothic formula to preclude terminal rewards: "There were the sufferings, the hero in the mask of a villain, the villain in the mask of a hero, the flights, the looming death, the sense of being imprisoned, but there was no happy ending, no true love" (p. 259).

Both these models of the heroine's text, the traditional and the inverted (and the "unhappy power" motif of the inverted version is at least as familiar, defining a dilemma that entraps characters ranging from the Lady of Shalott to Joan's own mother), present a myth of origins for the female "self" that stresses isolation and estrangement. Joan apprehends that the conclusions of such stories overlook something, leave out something important, and the various female bodies that haunt her while remaining invisible to the masculine gaze suggest that such societally sanctioned constructions of the female quest for identity are intended to limit a subversive multiplicity that, paradoxically, inheres in the feminine Other precisely because that Other is defined in opposition to the unified, phallic self.

In other words, the threat of the feminine derives from the fact that it is defined by an act of marginalization, by a thrusting of "woman" to a position outside the order of the Same. Because she has been constructed not as self-same but as utterly different, she resists gestures of unification that belatedly attempt to control the implications of her Otherness. In *Lady Oracle*, a number of the female characters have more than one identity, or an identity that in some respects contradicts the received wisdom about possible combinations of power and happiness. Joan's mother tries to dismiss Aunt Lou, for instance, as "bitter and frustrated because she didn't have a huband," but Joan reflects, "To me she seemed a lot less bitter and frustrated than my mother, who, now that she'd achieved and furnished her ultimate house, was concentrating more and more of her energy on forcing me to reduce" (p. 88). Aunt Lou seems to be conducting a pleasant and stable relationship with a married man and has a job with a sanitary napkin manufacturer that significantly puts her in charge of one of the most unsanctioned aspects of female sexuality, menstruation, and makes her an authority on female maturation and reproduction, whereas Joan's mother has internalized the terms of her own constriction to become an authority only on reduction.[26]

Similarly, the disorientingly named Leda Sprott, the cult leader who seems to have put on a version of Olympian knowledge and power without having to suffer Olympian rape, is reincarnated as the Reverend Eunice P. Revelle and empowered to perform legal marriages despite the fact that the new identity arose from an evasion

[26]See my "Writing—and Reading—the Body: Female Sexuality and Recent Feminist Fiction," *Feminist Studies* 14 (Spring 1988), 121–42, for a more detailed examination of menstruation as a conventionally unrepresented aspect of female sexuality (along with urination, defecation, and giving birth). Joan discovers the evidence of her mother's "terrible anger" only after her mother's death, in a photograph album where all the faces of the men have been razored out. She immediately identifies the rage with the constriction of her mother's identity: "I could almost see her doing it, her long fingers working with precise fury, excising the past, which had turned into the present and betrayed her, stranding her in this house, this plastic-shrouded tomb from which there was no exit" (p. 201).

of the law ("Leda Sprott owes a little money here and there," she confides to Joan [p. 231]). Loosely associated with the prepatriarchal mystery religion figure of the Great Mother, whose home was the subterranean labyrinth,[27] this doubled Fat Lady has—and can discern in Joan—powers, capacities in the plural. Like Aunt Lou, she tends to utter prophecies that in the best oracular tradition are wholly ambiguous, subject to at least two contradictory interpretations. Central among these is the injunction that forms part of her eclectic wedding ceremony: "Avoid deception and falsehood; treat your lives as a diary you are writing and that you know your loved one will someday read, if not here on this side, then on the other side where all the final reconciliations will take place" (p. 227). This platitude, like the fortune cookie messsage *"It is often best to be oneself"* (p. 257), seems to be part of a system of adjurations supporting the popular notion of a female "self" lurking underneath the various alternative identities that must be dimissed as false. But in both cases the message is complicated by context: the recipient of the fortune cookie is not Joan but the "paragon" Marlene, and the speaker who urges that Joan "avoid deception and falsehood" is operating under an assumed name. Moreover, the notion that Joan's life is a "diary . . . that you know your loved one will someday read," resonates insidiously at the conclusion of the novel, when the story of Joan's life is revealed to have been "told to" a male ghost writer and to contain lies. The presumption of an eventual audience appears to dictate more, rather than less, invention.

Joan's mother stands in implicit opposition to these multiple and physically excessive female characters, and Joan represents her mother's whole life as one of self-restraint in the expectation of an eventual reward: "She used to say that nobody appreciated her, and this was not paranoia. Nobody did appreciate her, even though she'd done the right thing, she had devoted her life to us, she had made her family her career as she had been told to do, and look at us" (p. 200). In her "astral" manifestations, this mother always appears the way she looked in Joan's childhood: around thirty years old, rigorously girdled, and "colored in" with cosmetics. But it is

[27]Atwood discusses the myth of the Great Mother and her association with the labyrinth in the interview with Cathrine Martens. Godard works especially with this myth, and with the Demeter/Persephone myth, in "My (M)other, My Self."

this manifestation that the child Joan initially perceived as misleadingly narrow, an arbitrary reduction of her mother's multiplicity, which she tried first to shield from, then to expose to, the masculine gaze:

> Although her vanity tables became more grandiose as my father got richer, my mother always had a triple mirror, so she could see both sides as well as the front of her head. In the dream, as I watched, I suddenly realized that instead of three reflections she had three actual heads, which rose from her toweled shoulders on three separate necks. This didn't frighten me, as it seemed merely a confirmation of something I'd always known; but outside the door there was a man, a man who was about to open the door and come in. If he saw, if he found out the truth about my mother, something terrible would happen, not only to my mother but to me. I wanted to jump up, run to the door, and stop him, but I couldn't move and the door would swing inward. . . .
>
> As I grew older, this dream changed. Instead of wanting to stop the mysterious man, I would sit there wishing for him to enter. I wanted him to find out her secret, the secret that I alone knew: my mother was a monster. (p. 70)

The dreams about her mother's hydra-headedness and the man on the "other side" of the door are structurally analogous to the Gothic recognition scenes that Joan first writes and then enacts near the close of the novel. Moreover, the mirrors that allow her mother to make herself into the requisite object of masculine desire, and thus to make herself into an exemplary mirror that will reflect back exactly what the phallocentric culture wishes to see, are transformed by the dream into portals leading to the revelation of feminine monstrosity, of woman as irreducibly multiple. In Joan's experiments with automatic writing, the triple mirrors lead into a labyrinth identified both with the unconscious and with the maternal.

As Claire Kahane has noted, the Gothic heroine negotiates the labyrinth in order to leave it behind. Her discovery of her "self" at the center of the maze allows her to transcend the maze altogether in a final repatriation that isolates her forever from the twinings of a seductive and dangerous femininity. In *Lady Oracle*, however, the Gothic quest is travestied in the account of a Brownie rite of passage:

> You . . . had to close your eyes and be turned around three times, while the pack chanted,
>
> Twist me and turn me and show me the elf,

I looked in the water and there saw . . .

Here you were supposed to open your eyes, look into the enchanted
pool, which was a hand-mirror surrounded by plastic flowers and
ceramic bunnies, and say "Myself." The magic word. [p. 64]

At the center of the twistings and turnings, the place of the self, is
a mirror, single this time. But what does it mean that the self is
identified with a mirror?

In the opening passage, Joan had bewailed her failure in these
terms: "My life had a tendency to get flabby, to scroll and festoon
like the frame of a baroque mirror." The reserve and self-effacement
of a frame, which both supplements and sets boundaries for the
thing it is framing, is here betrayed specifically as a failure of mirroring: the border that scrolls and festoons distracts from the primary
business of reflection. The simile may recall Irigaray's discussion of
the posited feminine as a flat mirror, simultaneously the product
and the maintenance of the order of the Same, that "old dream of
symmetry."[28] In *Lady Oracle*, Joan relates her life as a series of attempts to be an exemplary mirror to the masculinist culture, reflecting back only what she is called upon to reflect. But despite what
she represents as her best efforts, the enterprise is self-sabotaging.

First of all, it turns out that in order to be an ideal reflector she
must sustain several completely separate identities: nurturing and
bubble-headed wife, shy and middle-aged author of mass-market
fantasies for women, kinkily sexy quondam mistress, and exotic and
otherworldly cult "poetess." The multiple identities are necessary
precisely to sustain the myth of her own accessory status—her own
supplementarity and thus her own deficiency.

Second, it turns out that the mirror is the vehicle for the recognition of her own radical plurality. Looking in it to find "Myself,"
Joan finds instead another labyrinth, itself the distorted double of
the maze in *Stalked by Love*, and enters it only to come out with
another identity, the "dark twin" of the poem "Lady Oracle." In
this novel, mirrors confirm not the unity of the self but the difference
inherent in the operation of reflection, and this difference opens up

[28]The opening chapter of *Speculum of the Other Woman*, on Freud's treatment of
female sexuality as the symmetrical complement of both male sexuality and male
desire, is titled "The Blind Spot of an Old Dream of Symmetry" (pp. 11–129).

the possibility of dis-integration, of subversive and perhaps even salvific multiplicity. Luce Irigaray has noted how the Cartesian subject of *cogito ergo sum* discovers—on *reflection*—that he is thinking, and makes of this mirror image a founding certainty. But observing how the *cogito* splits the self into thinker and thought-of only to suture up the split before it can be acknowledged, she asks, "What if, therefore, the crucial thing to do were rather, or especially, to conclude that the *other* exists?"[29] Joan is continually adjured to "be yourself," but in Atwood's novel being yourself is a trick done with mirrors, a feat requiring coincidence with a reflection that is unalterably other. She must *be* what *is seen*, and only that; and if the demand implies an impossible act of self-annihilation, it is consonant with what fashion magazines, for example, urge on young women as a matter of course. And ironically, this adjuration to become solely the visible self is fully consonant with the privileging of visibility and the sole phallus in the judgment that defines the condition of femininity as one of castration: *nothing to be seen*.

But what if "no-thing" meant a number of things, a number of identities, for example, or even a number of irreconcilable "truths" about the relation of femininity to masculinity? After Joan has conducted her heroine, Charlotte, to the center of the maze and concluded that the conventional resolution involves "a wrong turn somewhere" (p. 366), she enters the maze again, this time in the persona of her Gothic alter ego, the wife and villainness Felicia. Stumbling into the center, Felicia comes upon a collection of her own—and Joan's—avatars: two women who look "*a lot like her, with red hair and green eyes and small white teeth*," one who looks like Aunt Lou and one who is clearly the Fat Lady and who wears not only the tutu and the pink tights of Joan's fantasies but, in an allusion to one of the most painful incidents of Joan's childhood (pp. 43–52), has "*two antennae, like a butterfly*" sprouting from her head and "*a pair of obviously false wings . . . pinned to her back*" (p. 375). Having ascertained that all these women are, as she is, Lady Redmond, Felicia arrives at the culminating revelation the labyrinth offers: "*Every man has more than one wife. Sometimes all at once, sometimes one at a time, sometimes ones he doesn't even know about*" (p. 376). Yet it is

[29]Irigaray, *Speculum*, p. 183 (my emphasis).

precisely in their revealed multiplicity that these wives have become void for Redmond. The labyrinth that throughout the development of the plot has been associated with the threat of an entangling and potentially unresolvable femininity (*"Some say as how there's no center to the maze,"* reports one of the novel's faithful retainers [p. 209]) has become a means of containment and ultimately of eradication. Felicia realizes that she is *"trapped here with these women. . . . And wasn't there something peculiar about them? Wasn't their skin too white, weren't their eyes too vague?"* (p. 376). Furthermore, she cannot turn back: " *'Back?' said the first woman. 'We have all tried to go back. That was our mistake.'* " After such knowledge, the only possible return is to the husband who can now be revealed as the man who is trying to kill her.

But the central "truth" of this imbedded story—that all men are killers who dread, and for this reason menace, female multiplicity, forcibly reducing it to no-thing—is immediately evaded, for the imbedded story is not the truth of the novel. Or not the only truth of the novel: by this time the whole convention of imbedding has become as unresolvable as the centerless maze. In fact, it is increasingly unclear, as *Lady Oracle* scrolls and festoons into its conclusion what, exactly, is the "real" story and what strands of plot may be subsumed as inventions, fantasies, projections, or hallucinations. Contemplating possible endings for *Stalked by Love*, Joan reflected earlier,

> I knew what had to happen. Felicia, of course, would have to die; such was the fate of wives. Charlotte would then be free to become a wife in her turn. But first she would have to have a final battle with Redmond and hit him with something (a candelabrum, a poker, a stone, any hard sharp object would do), knocking him out and inducing brain fever with hallucinations, during which his features and desires would be purified by suffering and he would murmur her name. She would nurse him with cold compresses and realize how deeply she loved him; then he would awaken in his right mind and propose. [p. 348]

The last chapter of *Lady Oracle*, when Joan confesses to having knocked out the man on the other side of the door with a Cinzano bottle and adds, "There's something about a man in a bandage" (p.

379), flirts with this conclusion, as with the conventional conclusion of the genre "nurse novels" written by Paul, the Polish Count. But here the man in a bandage is an altogether new stand-in for the hero, a development that makes purification through suffering beside the point. The conventions are so haphazardly applied, in fact, that this ending might belong to a completely different novel—or it might be the beginning of a completely different novel. Narrative multiplicity has not resolved unambiguously into unity. Instead of a recognition, a final moment of self-coincidence, Joan seems once again to disperse, this time into plans for more stories, presumably involving more authorial personae, and into her throwaway disclosures about the reporter's mediation and her own lies. Indeed, the lengthy "rising action" of the classical plot has been betrayed by the lack of a climax—or by the fact that the climax is at the very least difficult to locate, recurring, diffuse; as if the model of plot construction here were something more polymorphous and perverse.

In this calculated miming of "the feminine" as a condition of essential deficiency, Atwood has in effect created an alternative narrative structure, a structure that in important ways is not modeled on masculine sexuality (as is the "classic" linear and teleological plot, with its situation, rising action, climax, and denouement) and that resists the masculinist ideologies encoded in the "classic" structure by refusing to make a univocal revelation the point of the whole story, in this way refusing to privilege a single version of "the truth" as definitive. Like female desire in this novel, the central questions are developed only to resist containment and unitary embodiment, and as a consequence they remain disconcertingly present, bobbing like gloriously inflated Fat Ladies above any ostensible resolution.

IV

Lady Oracle emerges from this discussion as a prime example of representation with a difference, a novel in which the Other Woman makes herself known through ruptures and dislocations of the economy of the Same. Yet difference can always be read as no-thing— and indeed was read this way when *Lady Oracle* first came out. The following quotations are from two major reviews:

It may be that the genre [of "popular feminist-oriented fiction"] is not congenial to Atwood's real gifts: perhaps the very confusion of "Lady Oracle" is a measure of her discomfort.

The novel does not develop, it meanders, circling around and turning on itself—letting its contours be defined by the chaos of the heroine's psyche.[30]

In the first quotation, the feminine deficiency is ascribed directly to the writer: *Lady Oracle* is "confused," because Atwood is "confused" (although the reviewer tries to mitigate the criticism by making an unfortunate choice of genre the source of Atwood's "discomfort"). In the second quotation, the feminine deficiency is ascribed, more flatteringly, to the writer's creation, and Atwood is credited with having *invented* (presumably for some ethical or therapeutic purpose) a woman whose psyche is in "chaos"—that is, a woman whose essence is deficiency or lack. In either case, both the self and the narrative are presumed to be aspiring toward a familiar model of coherence, and dis-unity is read as somebody's failing: predictably, as the failing of some woman.

It is not surprising that *Lady Oracle* can be read back into the discourse of the Same—can be read as an attempt to emulate a patriarchally constructed order, an attempt that in various ways and for various reasons fails to live up to the masculinist standard and so emerges as merely *dis*ordered: characterized by "confusion," "chaos," a structure that "does not develop, it meanders." Each of the chapters in this book has begun from a survey of existing criticism on the writer under discussion. In each case, the main tendencies of the criticism suggest that readings reinscribing feminist writing in the order of the Same are historically the easiest and the most accessible readings, even when they misconstrue or falsify elements of the fiction they purport to explain. In each case, even the dominant feminist readings work against the acknowledgement of conscious innovation and experimentation on the part of feminist writers. In many respects, it appears that the novice reader's question, "What is she trying to say?" has been granted unique relevance to feminist narrative. Of course, "trying to say" is an untenable

[30]Katha Pollitt, *New York Times Book Review*, 26 September 1976, 7–8; LeAnne Schreiber, *Time*, 11 October 1976, 98.

formulation, implying as it does not only a "trying" that falls short of complete success (thus the reader must "say" what the author was incapable of articulating) but also a theory of writing as an unproblematic "saying" subsequently cloaked in language (thus the reader's job is to disentangle meaning from the duplicitous veils of rhetoric in which it is swathed).

The question remains whether such reductive readings are inevitable—whether when difference speaks, it can be heard, and if it can be heard, how one might learn to listen for it. In a passage from her essay "This Sex Which Is Not One," Irigaray writes, "One would have to listen with another ear, as if hearing *an 'other meaning' always in the process of weaving itself, of embracing itself with words, but also of getting rid of words in order not to become fixed, congealed in them.*"[31] In the context of contemporary feminist narrative, I find this notoriously difficult description both lucid and revelatory. "Listening with another ear" suggests attunement to a project involving representation with a difference, representation that generates an elusive "other meaning" by questioning, subverting, and parodying masculine models in the process of mimicking them. Such a project is inherently political and, furthermore, implies that politics is not divorced from issues of language. The political cannot be understood as an unmediated "saying," a communication of a "content" separable from "form."

Contemporary feminist narrative is both experimental and political inasmuch as it is characterized by pervasive parodies, mimicries, and subversions. My enterprise has been to suggest that if one listens with an ear not entirely attuned to the discourse of the Same, if one acknowledges that when difference speaks, its productions will deviate from—while still relying on—sanctioned modes of discourse, then the Other Side and the Other Woman become manifest as a ballooning of possibilities.

[31]Luce Irigaray, "This Sex Which Is Not One," in *This Sex Which Is Not One*, trans. Catherine Porter (Ithaca: Cornell University Press, 1985), p. 29.

Index

Library of Congress Cataloging-in-Publication Data

Hite, Molly, 1947–
    The other side of the story : structures and strategies
of contemporary feminist narrative / Molly Hite.
        p.   cm.
    Includes index.
    ISBN 0–8014–2164–0
    1. English fiction—Women authors—History and criticism.
    2. English fiction—20th century—History and criticism.
    3. Feminism and literature—History—20th century. 4. Narration
(Rhetoric) 5. Rhys, Jean—Technique. 6. Lessing, Doris May, 1919–
Golden notebooks. 7. Walker, Alice, 1944– Color purple
    8. Atwood, Margaret Eleanor, 1939– Lady Oracle. I. Title.
PR888.F45H58   1989
823'.914'099287—dc19   89–776